COVID-19

Impact on Education and Beyond

COVID-19

Impact on Education and Beyond

Editors

Nivedita Das Kundu

Aloysius Nyuymengka Ngalim

Vij Books India Pvt Ltd
New Delhi (India)

Published by

Vij Books India Pvt Ltd
(Publishers, Distributors & Importers)
2/19, Ansari Road
Delhi – 110 002
Phones: 91-11-43596460, 91-11-47340674
M: 98110 94883
E-mail: contact@vijpublishing.com
Web : www.vijbooks.in

ISBN: 978-93-90439-52-2 (Hardback)

ISBN: 978-93-90439-60-7 (Paperback)

ISBN: 978-93-90439-68-3 (ebook)

Dedicated to

Health Care Workers, Teachers and Learners

This Book is Published in Association with Bharat Centre of Canada (BCC).

Bharat Centre of Canada (BCC) is an independent non-partisan Policy Think Tank, focuses on understanding contemporary India and Canada – India Relations. BCC's objective is to bring out new vision and innovative ideas to work with Indian and Canadian counterparts. BCC looks forward to connect with the policy makers, academics, scholars, researchers, practitioners, diplomats of both India and Canada and establish collaborations overcoming the gaps and challenges. BCC maintains an interdisciplinary approach and provides an understanding on how to enhance the scope of cooperation and engagement between the two nations and increase people to people contact. BCC aims to focus on the existing collaborations and the factors that can underpin the success, as well as, identifies the bottlenecks. BCC also recognizes future possibilities and emerging opportunities. BCC promotes quality research and in-depth studies and is a platform for dialogue to promote initiatives that further the cause of peace and global harmony. With a team of dedicated academics, professionals and community members, this Policy think tank works closely with local partners and associates in India, Canada and in other countries to fulfil its stated objectives.

Mission

Mission is to become a premium resource hub on India in Canada, conduct in depth research, provide inclusive platform and invest in future prospects

Objective

Promote awareness and understanding, bring together policy makers, researchers, university/college students, academics, practitioners and business entities among others

Contents

List of Figures

Preface

The spread of the Coronavirus pathogen (COVID-19), made 160 countries or more, mandated provisional school closures. Extended school closures may cause not only loss of learning in the short-term, but also further loss in human capital and diminishes economic opportunities in the long-term. To help mitigate the loss of learning, many countries have and are pursuing options to utilize remote learning or e-learning to manage and cope with the crisis.

The spread of the new coronavirus in the spring of 2020 overturned almost all aspect of life. On March 11, as the infection navigated and crisscrossed the globe with contemptible speed, scale, and severity, the World Health Organization (WHO) declared COVID-19 a pandemic. As a result of this unprecedented decision, the lives of students all over the world have been adversely affected. Thereafter, nations began moving their curriculum online to ensure that students continued learning while at home unperturbed. In early April 2020, that is about, two months after WHO's declaration of COVID-19 as a pandemic, the joint initiative of Bharat Centre of Canada (BCC) and the Jadavpur Association of International Relations, (JAIR) Kolkata, India sent out a call for abstracts for an International Online Conference on 8th May 2020.The theme of the conference was, "Methods of Teaching and Learning used by the Educational Institutions during the Period of Lockdown due to COVID-19 Pandemic." Against this backdrop, a group of colleagues joined forces to publish a book addressing myriad questions about the coronavirus pandemic and learning. The decision to publish this book opened in a discussion of findings in the context of broader efforts in this online conference. Scholars in this book drew on their deep expertise to identify and examine a range of vital issues implicated by COVID-19. Mindful of the need to match the fast-moving impact of the virus, the authors worked at record speed to turn their analyses and insights into the essays that make up this collection, "COVID-19: Impact on Education and Beyond".

Weeks before the conference, what only months ago seemed an impossible achievement (implementing and enforcing austere quarantine measures and isolating millions of people) became a reality in many countries. People all over the world had no option than to adapt and invent new lifestyles. The twelve contributors to this book have diligently dilated on the important theme of "COVID-19: Impact on Education and Beyond." The contributions have corroborated the thesis that pandemics are a burgeoning area in global studies and are continuously growing, given that pandemics are sudden and dangerous. The book contains concrete suggestions for how to help students and teachers within the COVID-19 ordeals. It focuses on the impact of the pandemic on teaching/learning and psycho-social development. It has concrete suggestions at the micro and macro level for change, enabling students, educators and institutions to become pandemic-responsive. Described as a multidisciplinary and to an extent comparative investigation, it covers themes such as the teacher-student online interaction, economic hardships, health concerns, equity, access and inclusion, governance, partnership and collaboration, support services for special needs students, different models of course-delivery, evolution of medical therapy, and mass hysteria in the time of COVID-19.

As constructivist theories were embraced in the 1980s and 1990s, knowledge construction and sharing tools ascended to demonstrate vital ideas and principles. Anybody teaching or learning in the emerging learning technologies for the past few decades realizes that the topics of interest change like the wind. Attention has shifted to the use of shared online video for learning as well as flipped classrooms, virtual worlds like Second Life, open textbooks, and various forms of mobile learning. Rather than discussing teaching and learning in a decontextualized manner and detailing their thoughtful use in educational settings, the learning theories which the authors represent in this book, are specific education-COVID-19 initiatives, related problems and issues that they can help address. During this time, one thing was becoming increasingly clear, learning technologies were emerging and evolving at a much faster pace at the start of the twenty-first century than had ever been witnessed in the previous one. It was almost as if a magic switch went off toward the end of the 1990s to bid adieu to educational technology as we knew it and to signal the start of an era where such technology would not simply be used to enhance, augment, or extend human learning and intelligence, but potentially transform it in revolutionary ways not seen before (Bonk 2009a).

Despite all the exuberance for teaching and learning with technology during COVID-19, the world of educational technology is one that remains filled with caveats, concerns, and an assortment of unknowns. Some raise cautionary flags over the cost justifiability of different technology tools and applications. Others sound alarms over their practical implications. Still, others ask whose needs are being served and for what purposes countries adopt or integrate a particular technology tool or application into learning and teaching. Today, when much of the world is dealing with a global pandemic, a medley of prevalent tools for real-time connections like Zoom (Hogan and Sathy 2020; Snider 2020), Adobe Connect, Cisco WebEx, BlueJeans, Skype, Google Hangouts, and Facebook Messenger Rooms (Bonk & David 2020) has transformed the instructional capabilities of synchronous technology. Nowadays, blended learning is also popular unlike the late 1990s and early 2000s in instructional design and educational technology especially with the emergence of COVID-19 (Bonk & David 2020).

Because of the sudden shift to online schooling, concerns are raised about whether education systems are equipped for such a quick scale-up of digital learning. The book has policy implications as it shares experiences from four continents of the World especially the hurdles and opportunities within COVID-19 teaching and learning. The experiences shared in this book are geared towards empowering countries currently in the coping phase to manage school closures and prepare for managing learning continuity when schools open as well as, a third phase of resilience and reform to improve the system for the long run.

To help mitigate the loss of learning during COVID-19, this book has demonstrated how many countries are pursuing options to utilize remote learning to ventilate local realities, connect and fraternize with the global to manage and cope with the pandemic crisis. This book has therefore demonstrated new ways of conceptualizing pandemics from different continents as countries combined the global and the local with a variegated strategy based on their particular circumstances. In essence, the authors of this volume have reconceptualized pandemics with more methodological rigour and presented the COVID-19 crisis against multiple challenges in their everyday lives, particularly against a backdrop of seismic global socio-economic transformations. Given that pandemic studies are an increasingly blossoming and kaleidoscopic area of scholarship, perhaps researchers might undertake critical studies on the impact of pandemics on teaching and learning, above all, learners/teachers and virtual learning that is cumulatively creating a new global generation in a digital era.

As such, this special issue should have massive appeal to graduate students and those early in their post-graduate careers looking for research topics to explore during their graduate studies and beyond. It should simultaneously appeal to more senior researchers and scholars who are seeking to understand how these fields have evolved in terms of the research as well as, where the open gaps in the research remain. This book can help colleges reopen thoughtfully and responsively whether remote or in person. It certainly qualifies for this list!

–Aloysius Nyuymengka Ngalim

References

Bonk, C. J., & David A. W. (2020). "Preface: Reflections on the Waves of Emerging Learning Technologies." *Education Tech Research Dev.* 68:1595–1612. https://doi.org/10.1007/s11423-020-09809-x

Hogan, K. A., & Sathy, V. (2020). 8 Ways to be more Inclusive in your Zoom Teaching. The Chronicle of Higher Education. Retrieved from https://www.chronicle.com/article/8-Ways-to-Be-More-Inclusive-in/248460. August 22, 2020.

Snider, M. (2020). Zoom Boosts Security Features, Encryption Amid Coronavirus Crisis Video Conferencing Boom. The USA Today. Retrieved from https://www.usatoday.com/story/tech/2020/04/22/coronavirus-crisis-drives-zoom-use-new-upgrade-increase-security.

Acknowledgements

This book is the result of an attempt to initiate greater understanding on the topic of "Methods of Teaching and Learning used by the Educational Institutions during the Period of Lockdown due to COVID-19 Pandemic," through an online conference organised jointly by Bharat Centre of Canada (BCC) and the Jadavpur Association of International Relations (JAIR), on 8th May 2020. This book owes its existence due to the support and encouragement by academics, scholars, and practitioners from nine different countries, whom all participated in the online conference during the difficult lockdown (pandemic) time and contributed their valuable thoughts and knowledge on the topic and shared their research chapters after the conference.

I would acknowledge the great support provided by my colleague from JAIR, Prof. Iman Kalyan Lahiri, who also ensured that this conference takes place with eminent experts, professors, and researchers from different countries. Without his support organising an online conference on such short notice with experts from different countries with different time zones would not have been possible. I would also like to acknowledge the unwavering support and encouragement by Maj. Gen. B.K. Sharma, Director United Services Institution of India, was also a keynote speaker of the conference. I would also like to thank Gp. Capt. Dr. Ajey Lele from Manohar Parrikar Institute of Defence Studies and Analyses for Chairing the conference and later contributing a chapter despite his busy work schedule. It would not be out of place to thank our health care sector front line worker, doctor Jayanta Das, vascular surgeon, and medicolegal expert, who shared primary source information about India's pandemic situation. He also contributed a chapter depicting his valuable thoughts despite being an extremely busy physician. No words would suffice to express my gratitude towards my colleague Ms. Ramneek Sidhu, who was incredibly supportive in conducting this online conference. She also helped in moderating and providing technical support.

I sincerely thank all the experts, eminent academics, scholars, and practitioners from different countries for their cooperative approach and research chapters' contributions. All the authors shared their insightful and thought-provoking ideas in their chapters. This book would not have been possible without the timely contribution from its eminent contributors, who submitted their valuable chapters on relatively lesser-known topics quite expeditiously despite their extremely busy schedule.

I also take this opportunity to thank my family members who were always there with their supportive and cooperative attitude for successfully conducting the virtual conference and later on to complete this edited volume. I would be grossly failing in my duties if I do not recognise my co-editor's contribution. I thank Professor Aloysius Nyuymengka Ngalim from the University of Buea, Cameroon, for his cooperation in the editing work. No words would suffice to express my gratitude for his sincere support to go through the drafts despite his busy university teaching schedule.

Last but not the least would like to take this opportunity to thank BCC & JAIR administrative and academic team, students, volunteers for their encouragement and cooperation. It is entirely due to all the contributors' wholehearted collaboration and assistance this volume has taken the present shape. I hope the readers find this book "COVID-19: Impact on Education and Beyond", that explores pandemic challenges and realities, useful, thought-provoking, and worthwhile.

–Nivedita Das Kundu

Editors and Contributors

Editors

Nivedita Das Kundu, Ph.D in International Relations. She is an academic with university teaching and think tank research experience. She is presently affiliated with York University, Toronto. Dr. Nivedita has completed her Master's and doctoral studies from Jawahar Lal Nehru University, New Delhi and University of Helsinki, Finland. She did her post-doctoral study from Woodrow Wilson Centre for Scholars, Washington DC. She has taught in prestigious Universities in Canada, Germany, Finland, India, Kyrgyzstan, Azerbaijan and worked in senior research positions with well-known government think tanks like Institute for Defence Studies and Analyses, Indian Council for World Affairs, Indian Council for Social Science Research, United Service Institution of India, Centre for Strategic Studies - Azerbaijan. She was a visiting fellow with Moscow State Institute for International Relations, Moscow State University, Russian Institute for Oriental Studies, Institute for International Relations, University of Kiev and School of International Relations, Sichuan University. She has authored two books and has been editor for seven books on International Relations. She has contributed research papers, articles to various research journals, websites and newspapers, chapters to edited Books. She has additional qualification on women, borders and migration studies from University of Hannover, and on Eurasian Studies from Pushkin State Russian language Institute. Her research expertise focuses on geopolitics, foreign policy, strategic dimensions of security, multilateral organisations, women and migration issues. Her accolades include prestigious state award "Pushkin Medal", in the year 2013. She has been the recipient of a number of prestigious fellowships DAAD (Germany), RAS (Russia), CIMO (European Union), ICSSR (India), ADA (Azerbaijan). She is also Chemical Weapons Convention Coalition member and works on WMD issues and concerns and participates regularly in CSP-OPCW, The Hague.

She is an adjunct faculty with United Service Institution of India & Birla Institute of Technology. She is in the editorial board of ethnic Canadian newspaper. She is a board member and chair working group, Science for Peace, University of Toronto. She is a President of Bharat Centre of Canada and an expert of Valdai Discussion Club, Russia.

Aloysius Nyuymengka Ngalim, Ph.D in History from the University of Nigeria, Nsukka. Dr. Aloysius is currently an Associate Professor, Department of History, at the University of Buea, Cameroon. He obtained MA magna cum laude and a PhD summa cum laude. He is a Fulbright Fellow and member of scholarly groupings such as the Council for the Development of Social Science Research in Africa (CODESRIA). He is CODESRIA's Multinational Working Group fellow. He is African Peacebuilding Network (APN), the Social Science Research Council (SSRC) grantee. He belongs to scholarly consortiums such as the African Network of Environmental Humanities (ANEH), and the Association of Friends of the Archives and Antiquities Cameroon (AFAAC). He is also consultant with United Nations Economic Commission for Africa (UNECA) on transboundary natural resources disputes in Africa. His research interests focus broadly on issues of agricultural and development history, heritage studies, youth and identity, child work and labour, conflict and mediation and culture in the third world. He has published scholarly papers in peer-reviewed journals in national and international journals, book chapters. He serves on the editorial boards of The Journal of International Relations (JAIR), Kolkata, India, Pan-Tikar Journal of History, Cameroon, Journal of African Politics and Society (JAPS), Nigeria and Peace and Conflict Studies Journal. He attended several conferences, workshops and symposia where he has presented papers on various themes. He is a Member of the University of Buea Committee for building University Institutional Repository (UBIR). He designs teaching and learning modules by applying learning principles and innovative strategies in instructional design for digital and other learning modalities for MA and PhD students in the Department of Curriculum Studies and Teaching, Faculty of Education. He teaches faculty who are new to teaching in online and blended formats.

Contributors

Sheriff F. Folarin, Ph.D in International Relations, is a Professor of International Relations and current Head of Department of Political Science and International Relations at Covenant University, Ota, Ogun State, Nigeria. Dr. Folarin was Director of the International Office and Linkages at Covenant University. He is currently the Chairman of the Board of African Leadership Development Centre (ALDC). He is the author of "Visibility and Relevance in International Politics: National Role Conceptions", and "Nigeria's Policy in Africa". His research interest includes international politics, foreign policy, global governance, media and development, gender and health diplomacy. He is Fulbright scholar and a former Visiting Fellow at the Walker Institute of International and Area Studies, University of South Carolina.

Ayodele Olaniyi, Lecturer, Covenant University, Ota, Ogun State. Nigeria. Ph.D. Candidate in Policy and Strategic Studies. He completed Bachelor of Science and Master of Science in Policy and Strategic Studies Covenant University, Ota, Ogun State, Nigeria. He has published research articles in peer-reviewed research journals. His areas of research international politics, foreign policy, global governance, media and development, gender and health diplomacy.

Fotini Bellou, Ph.D in War Studies, King's College London. Teaches in the Department of International and European Studies at the University of Macedonia in Thessaloniki. She holds Masters in International Relations from the University of Kent. Dr. Fotini also teaches in the Interdepartmental Joint MA progamme on 'International Relations and Security' with the Supreme Joint War College in Thessaloniki, and she is visiting Instructor to the Multinational Training Centre for Peace Support Operations at Kilkis, Greece. She is Special Advisor to the NRDC-GR in Thessaloniki on civil-mil cooperation and gender aspects and is a member of its civilian cell. She was Research Fellow with the Hellenic Foundation for European and Foreign Policy. She is managing editor of the Journal of Southeast European and Black Sea Studies, (Taylor & Francis). She has published on transatlantic relations, European and international security, aspects of conflict resolution and international relations and of international politics on South-eastern Europe.

Jayanta Das, MBBS, F.MAS, Dialysis Access & Peripheral Vascular Surgeon. He is a practicing surgeon in AMRI Hospital, Kolkata, India. Dr. Das is a course coordinator, PGDPML; WB NUJS. He is course coordinator in healthcare mediation, NLSIU (Bangalore). He is course director of FMLE, FNLE, WMLM (LUC Malaysia). He is the review committee member of "Malaysian Journal of Medical Research". He is general secretary of Dillon's kidney foundation. He is also Director of Dillon's medicolegal consultancy services.

Brenda Nachuah Lawyer, Ph.D in Curriculum Studies and Teaching from the University of Nigeria, Nsukka. Dr. Brenda is Senior Lecturer at the Faculty of Letters and Social Sciences, University of Douala, Cameroon. She holds Master of Education in Curriculum Studies and Teaching from the University of Buea Cameroon. She has held educational administrative positions. She is Chairperson for the Committee for the fight against Corruption for HTTTC (ENSET) Kumba. She has published widely within her scope of competence. Her research interest includes educational technology, comparative and global studies, education policy and social analysis, the science of education, inclusive education, pedagogy, administration, curriculum development and implementation, environmental education.

Shu Emmanuel Ngwa, Ph.D in Educational Policy and Administration from the University of Buea, Cameroon. He is M.Ed. in Comparative & Int'l Education from the University of Nigeria, Nsukka. Dr. Shu is currently an international contract staff at Alex Ekwueme Federal University Ndufu-Alike, Ebonyi State, Nigeria and lectures Educational Management at the Faculty of Education. He has published academic papers in international peer-review academic journals. His areas of research interest include higher education management, policy issues, school leadership & administration, inclusive education, sustainability education, comparative education, international education, education & development and teacher education.

Sandeep Poddar, Ph.D from the University of Calcutta. Dr. Sandeep is Senior Research Director and Executive Editor (Publications). He is also Member of Board of Studies, Lincoln University College, Malaysia. He is Masters in Zoology with specialisation in Biochemical Genetics from Dayalbagh Educational Institute. He is Assistant Secretary and Founder member of Dr. Tarak Nath Podder Memorial Foundation in Kolkata.

Ajey Lele, Ph.D from School of International Studies, Jawaharlal Nehru University, New Delhi. Dr. Lele is Senior Fellow in the Manohar Parrikar Institute for Defence Studies and Analyses and heads its Centre on Strategic Technologies. He started his professional career as an officer in the Indian Air Force. He has a Master's degree in Physics from Pune University. Group Captain Lele's areas of research include issues related to weapons of mass destruction, space security and strategic technologies. He has contributed articles to various national and international journals. He has authored six books and has also has been an editor for six books. He is a recipient of K. Subrahmanyam Award in 2013, conferred for outstanding contribution in the area of strategic and security studies.

Taghreed ElGhandour, **Ph.D** in Economics. She is teaching at the University. Dr. Taghreed is also an Advisor in the Ministry of International Cooperation, Egypt. She is a Fulbright scholar. She was an intern in FORMAPER, Agency of Milan Chamber of Commerce Industry Craft and Agriculture, International Relations Department, responsible for the implementation of technical assistance projects in the field of SMEs development all over the world. She also worked as a Co-trainer in several workshops about the strategic management of Official Development Assistance (ODA). Dr. Tagreed took part in different Programs; "The Political Economy of Football", European University Viadrina, Germany; "Governance in Africa", Residential School in Ghana, SOAS University of London, Mo Ibrahim Foundation; "Preparing Global Leaders Institute" Fon University, Macedonia and "Introduction to Entrepreneurship", Euro Mediterranean Training School, Venice International University, Italy.

Abbreviations

ACES	The Arab Campus E-Learning System
ASEAN	Association of South East Asian Nations
BRICS	Brazil, Russia, India, China and South Africa
CAD	Canadian Dollar
CCB	Canada Child Benefit
CAM-EDUC	Cameroon Education
COVID-19	The Coronavirus
CRTV	Cameroon Radio Television
CTC	Culturo-Techno-Contextual
EI	Employment Insurance
EELU	Egyptian E-learning University
GCE	General Certificate of Education
GEMR	Global Education Monitoring Report
GST	Goods and Service Taxes
GIS	Guaranteed Income Supplement
H5N1	Highly Pathogenic Asian Avian Influenza
ICT	Information and Communication Technology
ICTP	Information and Communication Technology Project
IGNOU	Indira Gandhi National Open University
IMF	International Monetary Fund
LMS	Learning Management Systems

MRC	Multimedia Resources Centres
MOETE	Ministry of Education and Technical Education
MOOC	Massive Open Online Courses
NEEP	National Education Emergency Plan
NGO	Non-Governmental Organisations
NCC	Nigerian Communications Commission
NELC	National E-Learning Centre
ODL	Open and Distance Learning
OECD	Organisation for Economic Co-operation and Development
PPE	Personal Protective Equipment
RTE	Right to Education
SCO	Shanghai Cooperation Organisation
TVET	Technical and Vocational Education and Training
UN	United Nations
UNDP	United Nations Development Project
UNESCO	United Nations Educational Scientific and Cultural Organisation
UNICEF	United Nations Children's Fund
UCM	Understand, Control and Manipulate
USDLA	The United States Distance Learning Association
WTO	World Trade Organisation
WHO	World Health Organization
WUR	World University Ranking

Introduction

Nivedita Das Kundu

Education is not only a fundamental human right; it is the key driver of sustainable development and progress. When the education system breaks down, then the growth and peace cannot be sustained in any society. The COVID-19 pandemic has pushed the world into the deepest global recession in living memory, that will have lasting effects on people's lives, in the education sector, economies and in the health care sectors. The coronavirus or COVID-19 started in Wuhan, China, in the second half of 2019, and gradually spread into other parts of the world. Within a few months, the virus became a global threat to human life and property. The COVID-19 pandemic affected all age groups and all sectors of societies. However, the impact of COVID-19 in the education sectors, the central theme of this book, has been unprecedented. The COVID-19 pandemic is already having a global impact on learners and teachers around the world, from pre-primary to secondary schools, technical and vocational education and training (TVET) institutions, universities, adult learning, and skills development establishments (United Nations, 2020) all were impacted due to the pandemic. There was a huge loss in the learning process and that might continue for a longer period than expected and affect the progress. Millions of children and youth from pre-primary to tertiary may drop out or not have access to schools in the next year or so due to the pandemic's economic slowdown. Similarly, disruption in the education process will have substantial effects beyond the education sectors too. Closures of the educational institutions also obstructed the provision of essential services to children and communities (United Nations, 2020).

This book focuses on teaching and learning during COVID-19. During the COVID-19 period, all levels of education and training are affected. The disruptions caused by COVID-19 to everyday life meant that millions of children worldwide have missed out on early childhood education in their critical pre-school years. They missed a stimulating and enriching environment, learning opportunities, social interaction and in some cases, adequate nutrition through daily snacks & food that is provided in many educational institutions. This is likely to compromise their long-term healthy development, especially those children from poor and disadvantaged families. In technical and vocational education and training systems, vulnerabilities including low levels of digitalisation and long-standing structural weaknesses, have been brought to light by the crisis. Disruptions in workplaces made it difficult to implement internships, training, co-ops and work-based learning modes, key elements of a functional and market-responsive technical and vocational options (United Nations, 2020). In the higher education sub-sector, while online learning has generally taken place through recorded lectures and online platforms, some universities have postponed learning and teaching until further notice, due to the lack of information and communication technology (ICT) infrastructure for both students and teachers.

As the health crisis unfolded, causing massive socio-economic disruptions, education systems around the world were swift to react and adapt. Governments responded quickly to ensure education continuity and protect the safety of learners and education actors by closing schools and other learning spaces. However, the unequal provision of learning modalities during closures will likely create inequities in the longer term. E-learning or online learning became the new normal during the pandemic. Though educational institutions were not prepared to convert into complete digitisation, technology gradually became the only solution in this "black swan" (an unpredictable situation with severe consequences) situation to overcome the volatility, uncertainty, and ambiguity.

During the pandemic time, international organisations fell apart. Instead of pursuing a collaborative approach to coping with the pandemic, the United Nations (UN) tried to politicise the cause of the pandemic, the World Trade Organisation (WTO) was confused and the World Health Organization (WHO) was at loggerheads. In an era where countries are increasingly drawn into an international system of exchanges, recently referred to as globalisation, the COVID-19 pandemic paradoxically is increasing the gap between developed nations with their fortress kind of mentality and developing nations creating an inter-state and intra-state migration problem thus, snowballing the politico-economic and social stresses. This attitude is seriously shredding the socio-economic structure and the so-called collaborative culture of the world. Leaders of most countries were overwhelmed with the unexpected pandemic crisis and to date, are struggling to deal with the ripple negative upshots. This situation has also become a security concern indicative of the fact that soft power is of equal importance as hard power. The pandemic has also made countries to realise the necessity to reduce defence budgets and rather stimulate the health sector to rejuvenate. Technology has become the most favourable option in the pandemic-stricken world with digital practices moving towards e-governance, e-health, e-learning, etc., to create a better technology-driven world.

This edited volume is the outcome of the international online conference titled, "Methods of teaching and learning used by the educational institutions during the period of lockdown due to COVID-19 pandemic." The online forum was jointly organised by the Bharat Centre of Canada (BCC), in collaboration with the Jadavpur Association for International Relations (JAIR) during May 2020. This book provides information and knowledge on the impact of the COVID-19 pandemic based on various parameters and how different nations are tackling the challenging situation. The well-researched chapters are written based on the practical experiences assessing the situation by prominent academics, practitioners, and university teachers from different countries.

The authors shared their expert views, provided their case study analyses of the existing situation of COVID-19, and put forward their recommendations. Thus, they ascertained the pros and cons of the pandemic measures especially on education as well as, the other domains of their countries. They went further to debate the topics of their research themes, focusing mainly on the teaching and learning process during the lockdown period and after the lockdown was lifted. The emphasis is on how the educational institutions got severely affected, how they were abruptly closed without a transition period to migrate to online classes. Since mid-March, most countries' governments declared lockdown especially as it affected almost all the primary, secondary, and higher education sectors. All the countries' governments tried their best to protect the learning process to keep students busy in order to curb or avoid delinquency due to idleness. In some countries, national television and radio stations were used for educational purposes. Virtual classrooms and online platforms became plausible and most appropriate means of teaching and learning during the pandemic time. Online platforms like Zoom, interaction with students through Moodle, Scribble, Big Blue Button, Google classroom, etc. became standard teaching methods.

While some educational institutions were prompt in introducing e-learning and provided adequate resources to the students, however, it was hard to cope with the new system for many educational institutions in some countries. As the learning process continued through various e-learning methods, some students were fast to cope up whereas, some faced difficulties in adapting to the new methods of learning. This is because not all students have access to technology and gadgets for online classes. Some countries' provincial and federal governments provided the students with facilities such as high-speed internet connections, laptops, tablets, and even online videos, documentaries, and audio files (in different languages) to make the online study possible and affordable to all. Nonetheless, it was not the same for all the students to concentrate through e-learning. Self-motivated students mainly managed to succeed, but many also faced difficulties. Overall, all the countries tried their best through various mechanisms and various degrees of successes to ensure that their education is reached to a significant number of students in order to continue learning while at home unperturbed. Analyses of the learning situation during COVID-19 shows that student's social skills were affected. However, the ability to work towards resilience and cooperation between the teachers and students increased. The chapters agree that though COVID-19 pandemic is creating challenges in the teaching and learning process, it equally ignites innovative reforms in the education system for better and increasing technology use. In many higher education institutions, the move to distance learning has been an opportunity to expand flexible learning modalities, setting the stage for a sustained shift towards more online learning in the future.

The chapters in this book pointed out that there are both short and long-term effects of e-learning. Today, the world is experiencing challenges, where century-old chalk and dusters are not the way of teaching, and digital learning has evolved as a practical option. The chapters highlight the fact that demands and criteria are not the same in every level of the education sector; for example, the elementary section aims to teach students behavioural education and focuses on the group activities to imbibe good behaviour in students like discipline, friendship, harmony, etc. Another important aspect is that in many elementary schools in some countries, mid-day meals are offered to provide healthy food to students and encourage education to the financially weaker sections of the society. Many elementary schools also try to develop leadership skills, bilingual proficiency, ethics, spirituality, and national identity. Through the online study programme, these essential aspects are missing. The chapters in this book articulated that online classes cannot be taken as an absolute measure in place of physical classes. During the pandemic time, all are trying to adapt to these new ways and methods, but the ongoing struggle for existence and survival for the fittest is continuing.

The chapters touched upon the disadvantages of online learning emphasising that there are many educational institutions in the world still not well equipped for digitisation and online learning. Many student's communities do not have digital facilities; many remote places do not have access to modern technology; hence, this technology-driven teaching and learning process creates a digital divide. This shortfall can largely be attributed to the digital divide, with the disadvantage of having limited access to basic household services such as electricity, a lack of technology infrastructure, and low levels of digital literacy among students, parents, and teachers. There are specific challenges faced by both developed and developing nations today. These are mainly accessibility and affordability of the digital platform, lack of training in e-learning and e-teaching, and electricity availability in many places. There is a central system of education in some countries, and in some countries, different provinces have different languages and different education systems. However, different strategies and methods were adopted during the pandemic time to facilitate the entire student's community to take care of their education, mental and physical health issues and concerns.

The researched essays in this book emphasise that skillfully crafted teaching and learning methods were introduced to benefit the student community. The inclusive learning process was encouraged so that vulnerable and marginalised societies should not get affected. The arguments given by the authors are that though it is understandable that online education cannot be adopted as the best option replacing physical teaching, but, for the time being, it is the most favoured option. It has been pointed out that the present situation taught how to handle any similar crisis if required, in the future, as many viable methods and options were learnt during this pandemic time. The chapters also touched upon the aspects that, to maintain the continuity in the learning process, many universities, colleges, institutes started holding regular online conferences and webinars. Social networking sites are used for effective collaboration during the pandemic time. Free literature from different countries' libraries and online lectures from different universities are regularly being shared with the students. It has been noted that teachers in various educational sectors are regularly helping students by motivating them in different ways to maintain a positive attitude; regular interactions with the students are taking place to avoid isolation and boost up their motivation level. Students' and teachers' collaboration showed a new approach to this relationship during the pandemic. The authors have highlighted that pandemic taught digital education has a good chance of growth and provided an excellent opportunity for many countries to speed up the digitisation process and increase the accessibility and affordability of reliable, high-speed internet facilities.

Students studying in foreign nations away from their home country faced severe problems during the pandemic time, as they were unable to get back to their home country due to sudden lockdown measures and due to the global travel restrictions. Uncertainty increased among the students, particularly regarding their student status. Many student's temporary resident visas expired. Many international students were feeling isolated and lonely due to uncertainty. Many were asked to vacate the university premises and many lost their part-time jobs. However, local community members managed to provide shelter, food, and basic necessities to those students.

Prior to the pandemic, certain universities had distance learning facility for students. The online learning process became much easier in those institutions. Many students interviewed mentioned that during the pandemic time, the transport cost and extra cost for recreation reduced but there were certain adverse effects too. For instance, the feeling of isolation, mental and physical health deterioration among others. Authors also pointed out that some teachers feel that online teaching is causing adverse effects among the teacher's community too. For example, going through regular online assignments and preparing for pre-recorded study materials made their job more time-consuming and sometimes tedious. Because of the lack of direct personal feedback from the students, the motivation level for teaching is going down in many teachers as the classroom atmosphere is different from the virtual atmosphere. Though online teaching and learning became essential, many departments like medical studies and other lab-oriented studies faced problems continuing with online education for a more extended period. Online teaching is suitable for theoretical teaching and learning, but it is not a viable option for practical classes. The chapters also highlighted that the younger population is in an advantageous position in e-learning compared with the older generations as older generations are comparatively less tech-savvy. Therefore, many adult education programs had to be cancelled during the pandemic time.

The idea that the democratic and inclusive nature of e-teaching provides a broader platform and gives teachers the independence to share their knowledge with the interested students freely is articulated in this book. The significant idea that emerges in the chapters is the need to do more to curtail the disadvantages of e-teaching like cybersecurity issues, internet connectivity problems, limited access to basic household services such as electricity, lack of technology infrastructure, and low levels of digital literacy among students, parents, and teachers. If these concerns can be taken care of, then, virtual teaching and learning would be an excellent option to transfer knowledge and skills. However, e-learning cannot replace the physical teaching and learning process.

This book is divided into three sections. The first section gives a broad overview on the teaching and learning experiences during the pandemic. The second section presents societal effect and schooling during the pandemic. The third section attempts to analyse e-learning and community concerns during the pandemic. Overall, the chapters in this volume touched upon various methods and options of teaching and learning as well as its impact on the societies during the pandemic time, providing insight into the reality. The theme of the chapters dexterously worked out with well-documented data based on the sources. The book on "COVID-19: Impact on Education and Beyond", has the potential to provide a broad idea and clarity on the crucial topic under study. The readers will find important information and understanding of how different countries tried to tackle the pandemic situation and how social life, economic and health situation impacted and teaching/learning processes continued during the difficult pandemic time. The book will provide readers with different viewpoints, concerns, and challenges of pandemic time from four continents of the world. It is expected that the book will fill the gap in the literature on this subject and provide useful inputs to policy planners.

Section I

Teaching and Learning Experiences During Pandemic

1

Classroom Beyond Borders: Teaching and Learning Strategies in Nigeria and Covenant University in the Global COVID-19 Lockdown

Sheriff F. Folarin & Olaniyi T. Ayodele

Abstract

For the first time in the world, a viral disease closes down the entire global system and collapses virtually all of human life everywhere. Unlike the Bubonic plague in the fourteenth century, Spanish Flu pandemic of 1918 and the H5N1, H1N1, SARS and Ebola of the 20th and 21st centuries; the coronavirus (COVID-19), because of its highly infectious nature, rapid spread, fatality rates- and more probably because of globalisation- has created an effective lockdown of economies and social life of about 90% of the world, which is unprecedented in human history. Educational institutions, particularly universities, are not left out. Social distancing to stem rapid community spread and a worsening fatal situation has been considered as an effective management or containment of the disease. It is for this reason that Nigerian universities have been shuttered since the middle of March 2020. Covenant University is not an exception. The institution was on first-semester break when the lockdown commenced; hence the students were locked not only out of the campus, but also out of Nigeria, for many- some were caught up in the United Kingdom, United States, Canada and United Arab Emirates. However, the lockdown has not stopped classes as the institution, Africa's fourth positioned University in the THE-WUR 2020 ranking, immediately activated and switched on its online platform. Zoom, contact with students on the interactive Moodle platform, Scribdle, Big Blue Button, among others, have been deployed for use or experimented with. This chapter discusses these coping mechanisms and strategies for teaching/learning, challenges faced and prospects in Covenant and attempts to identify the successes and shortcomings as far as impartation of knowledge is concerned. The participation-observation method is primarily useful, while direct interaction with colleagues and students as well as, feedback through the resources used, form the bulwark of the research instruments.

Introduction

The coronavirus pandemic locked down every facet of social life in Nigeria and the world. In Nigeria, the educational institutions, from primary to secondary schools, colleges of education, polytechnics and universities have been shuttered since the third week of March 2020. The highly infectious nature of the disease and rapid rate of spread necessitated the global lockdown of schools, organisations, pubs, cinemas, clubs, restaurants, parks and airports. The Nigerian authorities first shut down social life and non-essential movement in Lagos, Ogun and the Federal Capital Territory (Abuja). These -with Lagos leading the pack- were the initial epicentres, with the index case, being an Italian who had arrived in Nigeria two weeks earlier placed on intensive care. This was a development that warranted contact tracing and isolation of co-travellers on the flight as well as cab driver, cab driver's family members, co-workers and others (*This Day*, 2020).

The weeks that followed were chaotic, with lockdowns of major airports, transport system and limitation of movement effectively bringing a halt to associational or community living. School gates were shut and resumption of students and classes was not in view. Many Covenant University students, some of whom had travelled to the United States, United Kingdom, Canada and the United Arab Emirates for the first semester holiday, were locked out of Nigeria and could not return home. After a week and the lockdown seemed indefinite, Covenant University authorities switched to the online mode and commenced the second semester, using a number of mediums and resources to ensure that there were no gaps.

As resourceful as the online teaching and learning mechanisms seem to be, there have been challenges, ranging from human to technical, which underscores the importance or efficacy of physical contacts in teaching or learning. However, it is pertinent to mention that the present circumstances are desperate, which require drastic measures, such as going fully online in knowledge impartation. As stop-gap measures, the coping strategies have been useful, although it cannot entirely be like the regular teaching modules. The chapter discusses the coping strategies in teaching and learning at Covenant University since the COVID-19-induced lockdown of Nigeria's educational institutions. The specific measures, online tools or resources, the effectiveness of these tools and problems or challenges faced in the course of their deployment, are also discussed. The instrument of research is basically participation-observation. A number of academic staffs across the departments were randomly questioned and a proportional size of students was interacted with for feedback on the effectiveness or otherwise of the coping learning methods.

Global COVID-19 Pandemic and Lockdowns

The coronavirus disease first surfaced in Wuhan City, Hubei Province, China in late 2019. The disease is popular for its swift and deadly attack on and infection of the human respiratory system. The cause is described as Severe Acute Respiratory Syndrome Coronavirus 2 (SARS-CoV-2). Its novelty and exponential transmission across international borders made it pertinent for World Health Organization (WHO), the global public health policing body to designate it a global pandemic (Qian, Ren, Wang, Guo, Fang, Wu, Han and CPMA, 2020; WHO, 2020). The source of SARS-CoV-2 is still subject of many types of research but there are predictions pinning its source to animals and like the other coronaviruses, there is a possibility of its evolution from a virus that was previously found in animals (Anjorin, 2020). Coronavirus COVID-19 is the defining global health crisis of modern times and arguably the most threatening challenge the international community has encountered since the Second World War (UNDP, 2020). This virus is considered an existential threat, which has been linked to the infamous 1918 flu, with about 2.9 million confirmed cases as of September 2020, 196, 295 confirmed deaths and its presence in 213 countries, areas or territories globally (WHO, 2020).

The importance of physical distancing and lockdown orders in reducing the infection and death rate of the Global COVID-19 cannot be overemphasised; hence the adoption of these measures by different national governments. However, it has had a sizeable effect on socio-economic activities resulting in severe economic difficulties on national and global levels (IMF, 2020), resulting in job losses and hunger in many countries. Furthermore, the International Monetary Fund (IMF) has projected a 3% contraction in global income, assuming the different measures in place help curb or reduce to the barest minimum the pacing growth of the disease globally. UN (2020) has reported a multidimensional impact of the COVID-19 with emphasis on economy, learning, survival and health. However, the global governing body puts into consideration the uneven distributional effects of the coronavirus, especially in an era characterised by extreme inequality, predicting that children in the poorest countries, poorest households would be the worst hit.

Preparedness and response to the global pandemic have differed by countries, for reasons not farfetched. At the top of the factors is the obvious inequalities in areas of economy, health, governance, to mention a few, within the international community- while some can enforce total lockdowns giving their abilities to cushion the effects of the pandemic on their economy and citizenry, some are however limited to partial shuttering (Kaplan, Frias and Mcfall-Johnson, 2020). For instance, the Canadian government backed a C$107bn bill as emergency aid and economic stimulus to assist Canadians struggling financially because of the pandemic. Countries like India and Nigeria, giving their population figures, health inequalities, widening economic and social disparities and varying cultural values face more challenges in responding to the pandemic in line with best global practice (BBC, 2020; The Lancet, 2020).

The Community of Inquiry Model of Learning (CoL) and Online Learning

There have been theories of learning espoused to understand the place of different teaching environments in the cognitive test or enhancement of the adult in tertiary institutions. The Community of Learning (CoL) model of Garrison, Anderson and Archer (2000) is opposite in the context of the paper. The CoL model identifies three distinct "presences", namely cognitive, social and teaching components, with the submission that the three overlap and works contrapuntally. The CoL supports the design of online and blended courses as active learning marketplaces of knowledge, where teachers and learners interface. The CoL underscores the efficacy of online learning structures with the argument that as long as "social interaction" takes place (where there is a "presence"), the platform is a social community and learning can flow. This position is further strengthened in another study (Anderson, Rourke, Garrison and Archer, 2001) in which they argue that where there are discussion boards, blogs, wikis and video conferencing to set up and simulate a virtual space for a social interface between instructors and students, learning is as "social" as it can be in the physical classroom.

This model and argument are embraced by many scholars in the Information Communication Technology and Computer Science/ Engineering departments. Academics in these fields at Covenant University push to the limits the case for virtual classes and have in some cases, even long before COVID-19, advocated the use of online resources to teach in the entire semester. They had advocated learning by students from the halls of residence and teaching by lecturers from anywhere and writing of examinations only in a physical space (University Senate, 2018).

This study is not particularly interested in strengthening or otherwise, the position of online learning or teaching. It rather focuses only on what the coping online resources or strategies in this COVID-19 have been at Covenant University and how effective they are. The theoretical perspective of CoL merely underscores the growing importance of online-based learning in an age driven by information technology and how this has fitted the Covenant University context.

COVID-19 and the Nigerian Educational Sector

The outbreak and proliferation of the COVID-19 across global borders have had a multidimensional ripple effect on different countries. At the core of this is its severity on the health, economy and educational sectors (Oyetimi and Adewakun, 2020). Most national governments have embarked on the temporary closure of educational institutions. These nation-wide closures in about 186 countries (UNESCO, 2020) have impacted over 90% of the world's student population, which amounts to about 1.2 billion affected learners (73.8% of total enrolled learners). The localised closures implemented in other countries have further restricted access to education for additional millions of learners.

The world is fast embracing technological innovations in the form of e-learning and other remote access collaborative platforms to cushion the effect of the COVID-19 on countries, especially for continuity of educational activities. UNESCO has set a new standard and recommended its adoption for schools to employ distance learning programmes, open educational applications and platforms to reach learners remotely (UNESCO, 2020). The Federal Ministry of Education in Nigeria granted approval for the closure of Nigerian institutions for a one-month period on 19 March 2020, having recorded eight (8) confirmed cases of coronavirus in the Federal Capital Territory (Abuja), Lagos, Ogun and Ekiti states. This closure was timely and in line with best global practice at the time, as it was one of the initial approaches to curbing the spread of the virus globally (EiEWG Nigeria, 2020).

Migration to the digital space to continue educational activities should not be so difficult given that the world is currently driven by Information Communication Technology (ICT) and also considering the key objectives of the Nigerian national ICT policies, which primarily aims to convert Nigeria into a knowledge-based economy (National ICT Policy, 2012). The challenge, however, rests on the lagging nature of ICT development in Nigeria especially in areas of internet access, affordability and literacy. According to NCC (2019) Nigeria had recorded an estimated 122 million internet users and 33.13% broadband penetration as of May 2019. These figures, however, are low in comparison with countries who have relatively high levels of access to the internet in most developed countries and other regions, including Africa. Average access rate in North America and the Caribbean is 76.2%, Europe 80.2%, South America 65.3%, Oceania 69.6% and 47.0% in Africa (Leaning and Averweg, 2019).

Even though leading private institutions like Covenant University, Bowen University, among others, which are mostly ICT-driven institutions have immediately proceeded to internet-based learning, it is worthy of note that Academic Staff Union of Universities (ASUU), the apex body of the Nigerian academic community embarked on an indefinite strike from 23 April 2020. This was after the expiration of its initial warning strike, which was as a result of their rejection of the Nigerian government's decision to enroll them on the Integrated Payroll and Personal Information System

(IPPIS), a government's accountability software newly integrated into public institutions to manage the personnel payroll (Adedigba, 2020). The Ministry of Education, on the other hand, has commenced broadcast of educational programmes on major radio and television channels to further bridge the gap created by the scourge of the coronavirus pandemic and help basic and elementary school students to continue learning while at home (Mustapha, 2020). However, the difference in migration to online space in lower levels of education between public and private schools is also conspicuous. Unlike the Federal Government's plan to resort to broadcast learning, private schools have resolved to a totally different approach. Oyetemi and Adewakun (2020) reported that Greenspring's School, a notable British academy in Nigeria made an early decision to shut down and move all its early learning processes online. It is thus evident that many private institutions at all levels are prepared or equipped for the best global practice in online learning, which is mostly the use of remote interactive learning platforms.

Classroom Beyond Borders: Covenant University's Coping Strategies

Covenant University's resumption for the second semester in the 2019/2020 academic session was slated for 20 March 2020. However, this was disrupted by the COVID-19 outbreak and Federal Ministry of Education's order to shut all academic institutions across Nigeria for an initial one-month period (EiEWG Nigeria, 2020). Being a foremost citadel of learning in Nigeria and Africa and ranking somewhere between 401st and 500th in the world (THE-WUR, 2020), Covenant immediately sprang into action to see that academic activities continued even with the lockdown widely enforced in the country. Covenant University has maintained its reputation as a leading ICT-driven university in Nigeria since 2007 and this was evident in the prompt deployment of its e-learning platforms immediately physical resumption became impossible; hence, continuing the semester learning and teaching activities as scheduled. Covenant University's academic planning unit, powered by the school management immediately established communication with faculty and staff on the choice of the learning platform, one that would be able to provide real-time guidance on learning resources and support for students who would be learning from home.

Moodle Teaching Platform

Covenant adopted the Moodle teaching platform, also known as virtual learning environment in 2013- one that immediately attracted over 450,500 activities that same year and by a futuristic projection at the time, which would attract an estimated 2.5 million activities in the following semester (Covenant University, 2013). The virtual learning environment has since then remained a go-to place for students to receive lecture notes, take and submit assignments and quiz in form of tutorials, especially when reviewing topics.

Since the beginning of the lockdown, the use of the online platform has been maximised to include real time classes using the Big Blue Button addon, an open source web conferencing system for online learning (Moodle, 2008). Furthermore, this addon, which is preferably installed directly via the Moodle platform enables instructors to effectively engage students remotely, providing the learners and teachers with options such as real-time of sharing slides, audio, video, chats, to mention a few.

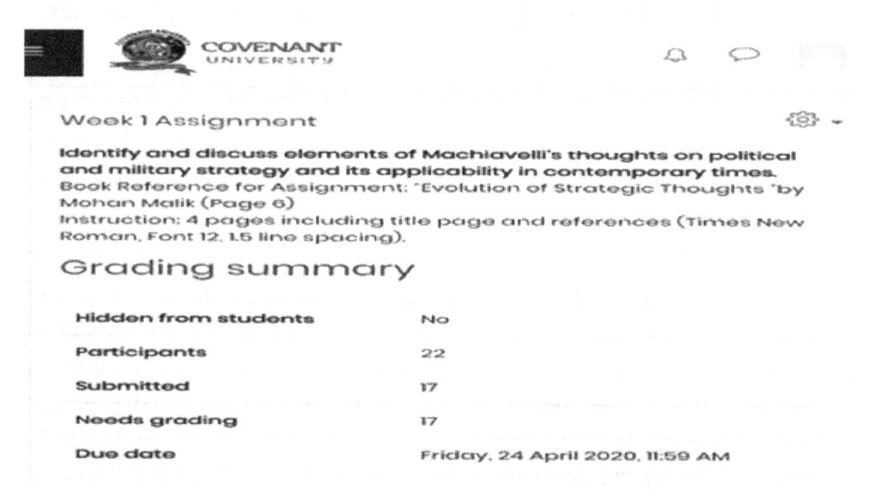

Figure 1: An image showing the assignment submission page on the Covenant University Moodle Platform

Students advisory and supervision also continue via ICT powered platforms, e.g. the university portal is equipped to capture students' course registration and proper documentation for usual semester activities, including health clearance, fees management, hostel allocation, and so forth. The University also encourages *in locos parentis,* which has enhanced the culture of good relationship and communication between faculty and students. These mediums have eased communication between project supervisors and research students, course advisers and students. The school management monitors the efficacy of the e-learning platforms by auditing site activities, gathering feedback from both students and parents, and also gathering progress reports through the department heads.

Figure 2: An image showing Covenant University's e-portal

Covenant's Challenges of Online Teaching and Learning

With an estimated 1.5 billion students out of the physical campuses and hundreds of millions migrating to the online space to continue learning, there have been new innovations and discoveries that have been projected to reshape academic process, learning methods and ultimately educational development in the 21st century (Anderson, 2020). Covenant University, known for its vast ICT infrastructure and deployment of tech-based academic learning solutions even before the pandemic, has maintained this reputation with its rapid migration to online based learning since it was faced with necessity of shutting its physical learning environment.

However, there has been a couple of challenges ranging from access to affordability since the online teaching and learning process commenced. According to Oyetemi and Adewakun (2020), adopting the online learning and teaching methods are welcome development, but the cost of access and sustenance of such have appeared to be a major challenge. Cost of accessing the internet remains exorbitant in Nigeria. In 2018, Oxfam revealed that the number of extreme poor in Nigeria had skyrocketed to 94.4 million people, with 3 million having been added to that unhappy lot in a span of six months, thus rating Nigeria at the poverty capital of the world for that year (Mailafia, 2019). Data cost should ideally be 2% of monthly income, which with N30, 000 ($77.58) minimum wage, should amount to N600 ($1.55) per 1 gigabyte. However, this is not reflective on the current data prices, as the average cost of 1-gigabyte data is N1,000 ($2.59) which is 66.67% increase in the price, which amounts to 3% of users' monthly income (Ekenimoh, 2019).

Covenant University like other schools, is also faced with the challenge of bandwidth consumption, even though the institution provides its faculty and staff with enough support in this regard. Students, who are however learning from home are exposed to the reality of expensive data rate and consumption as against what they experience while in school when they are on their monthly allocated quota measured to cover all their activities. Thus, Covenant also faces the challenges outlined by Oyetemi and Adewakun (2020) about parents who are primary caregivers of one or more children, bemoaning the bandwidth consumption and its impact on their purses, especially after they had paid tuitions.

Also, the technicalities of the e-learning platforms for both students and instructors as its hosted on the Moodle server, an online learning platform that hosts thousands of institutions. There have been complaints from both instructors and students of server failure on occasions. Another technical issue originates from signal strength, which is most important for efficient live interactions. Service disruption or poor network services can sometimes cause lagging in the interactions, which most times disrupt the activities, resulting in failed processes.

There is also another challenge that appears in form of online presence, which is important for online teaching and learning processes. Factors such as interruption or rotation of power supply, internet coverage, access and ultimately affordability on the parts of the students. Covenant University provides an optional accommodation service for its staff; those who should choose not to take this option are also subjected to the above factors, which means the constraints will also affect their capacity to be online.

Conclusions: Globalisation and the Future We See

There have been arguments in many enlightened circles that the increased and fast pace of movements across the globe has been the major factor in the spread of the virus. According to globalists, information and communication travel at the speed of light and in the same manner knowledge is quickly transmitted and, in the process, a universal global culture and "language" are created, which have reduced the global system into a compressed or "small" community of people or a global village.

Like global warming, climate change, drug and human trafficking, internet or cybercrime and terrorism; other dangerous trends and developments also move so quickly across the globe. But rather than the globalists pushing this as a frontier of their theory, the anti-globalists have been the ones making deposition that COVID-19 has become a global disease because of the globalising nature of human affairs or activities. The fast-pace movement, cross-cultural physical and social contacts, trade and commerce, tourism, sports, educational and cultural exchanges, among others, which have increased astronomically, have been used to explain away the global COVID-19 pandemic.

To these ends, with the known potential and real impact of globalisation -for good and for bad- nations of the world should live-ready. Governments should invest more and provide more online resources with other social infrastructure, such as ICT (Information and Communication technology) resources and sustainable electricity to enhance the capacity of educational institutions in worse-case scenarios as the COVID-19 pandemic. The Nigerian government has more to lose in view of its enormous population, in the event of a health pandemic as this. Its huge petrodollars could be utilised to provide the best ICT infrastructure in this information age, before oil fortunes dip further and become non-existent. University managements too should wisely invest in e-learning resources and begin to consider making online or internet-based learning a priority. COVID-19 has just shown the world the great alternative and dangers of not planning ahead.

References

Adedigba, A. (2020). ASUU begins 'Indefinite' Strike. Retrieved from: https://www.premiumtimesng.com/news/top-news/383371-just-in-asuu-begins-indefinite-strike.html on 29/04/2020.

Anderson, T., Rourke, L., and Garrison, D.R. (2001). Assessing Teaching Presence in a Computer Conferencing Context. Retrieved from https://auspace.athabascau.ca/bitstream/handle/2149/725/assessing_teaching_presence.pdf?sequence=1&isAllowed=y 04/05/2020.

Anjorin, A.A. (2020). The Coronavirus Disease 2019 (COVID-19): A Review and an Update on Cases in Africa. *Asian Pacific Journal of Tropical Medicine*, 13.

BBC (2020). Canada Backs $75bn Coronavirus Relief Bill. Retrieved from https://www.bbc.com/news/world-us-canada-52022506 on 27/04/2020

Covenant University (2013). Covenant University Consolidates ICT with e-Learning Platform. Retrieved from: https://covenantuniversity.edu.ng/layout/set/print/News/Covenant-University-Consolidates-ICT-With-e-Learning-Platform on 29/04/2020

EiEWG Nigeria (2020). Nigeria Education Sector COVID19 Response Strategy in North East. Retrieved from https://reliefweb.int/sites/reliefweb.int/files/resources/nigeria_education_sector_covid-19_response_strategy_north_east_.pdf on 29/04/2020

Ekenimoh, I. (2019). A Probe into the Expensive Cost Mobile Data Nigeria? *African Academic Network on Internet Policy*. Retrieved from: https://aanoip.org/a-probe-into-the-expensive-cost-mobile-data-nigeria/ on 29/04/2020

Garrison, D. R., Anderson, T., & Archer, W. (2000). Critical Inquiry in a Text-based Environment: Computer Conferencing in Higher Education Model. The Internet and Higher Education, 2(2-3), 87-105.

IMF (2020). World Economic Outlook. Retrieved from https://www.imf.org/en/Publications/WEO/Issues/2020/04/14/weo-april-2020

Kaplan, J., Frias, L., and McFall-Johnsen, M. (2020). A Third of the Global Population is on Coronavirus Lockdown. Business Insider. Retrieved from https://www.pulse.ng/bi/lifestyle/countries-that-are-on-lockdown-because-of-coronavirus/f28yp94 on 28/04/2020.

Lening, M. and Averweg, U. (2019). Dimensions of the Digital Divide. *Encyclopedia of Organizational Knowledge Administration and Technologies*, 3.

Mailafia, O. (2019). Poverty Capital of the World. *BusinessDay*. Retrieved from https://businessday.ng/columnist/article/poverty-capital-of-the-world/ on 05/05/2020.

Mustapha, T. (2002). COVID-19: Nigeria to bridge learning gaps via TV, radio programmes. Retrieved from: https://www.von.gov.ng/covid-19-nigeria-to-bridge-learning-gaps-via-tv-radio-programmes/ on 27/04/2020

Ogunmade, O., Ezigbo, O., Ajimotokan, A., James, S., Ogunje, V. (2020). Nigeria: COVID-19 - Italian Index Case Recovers, Discharged. Retrieved from https://www.thisdaylive.com/index.php/2020/03/21/covid-19-italian-index-case-recovers-discharged/ on 04/05/2020.

Oyetimi, K. and Adewakun, A. (2020). E-Learning: How COVID-19 is Reshaping Education in Nigeria. Retrieved from https://tribuneonlineng.com/e-learning-how-covid-19-is-reshaping-education-in-nigeria/ on 27/04/2020

Qian, X., Ren, R., Wang, Y., Guo., Fang, J., Wu, Z., Liu., Han, T., and CPMA (2020). Fighting Against the Common Enemy of COVID-19: a Practice of Building a Community with a Shared Future for Mankind. *Infectious Diseases of Poverty*, 9(34).

THE (2020). World University Ranking. Retrieved from: https://www.timeshighereducation.com/world-university-rankings/covenant-university on 29/04/2020

UN (2020). The Impact of COVID-19 on Children: Policy Brief. Retrieved from https://unsdg.un.org/resources/policy-brief-impact-covid-19-children on 27/04/2020

UNDP (2020). COVID-19 Pandemic: Humanity needs Leadership and Solidarity to defeat the coronavirus. Retrieved from: https://www.undp.org/content/undp/en/home/coronavirus.html on 27/04/2020.

UNESCO (2020). COVID-19 Educational Disruption and Response. Retrieved from https://unsdg.un.org/resources/policy-brief-impact-covid-19-children on 04/05/2020.

University Senate Meeting Deliberations, 21 May 2018.

WHO (2020) Coronavirus Disease (COVID-19) Pandemic. Retrieved from: https://www.who.int/emergencies/diseases/novel-coronavirus-2019 on 27/04/2002.

2

E-teaching in Greece at the Time of COVID-19: Opportunities and Challenges

Fotini Bellou

Abstract

The COVID-19 outbreak caused a series of changes in the education process worldwide. Schools, universities and colleges were closed while a number of novelties or certain adjustments to pre-existing distant teaching programmes were launched aiming not to severely discontinue the teaching semester schedule. Through a very short period of time, Greece had managed to coordinate a nation-wide e-teaching process in higher education which managed to complete the semester with only minimal disruptions. This chapter discusses and analyses the different methods of e-teaching that the University of Macedonia in Thessaloniki, Greece has been using following the lockdown of the country as a response to the COVID-19 pandemic. Although lockdown in Greece lasted for a two-month period, its aftermath did not bring students back to universities. Cautious measures favouring e-exams and the provision of electronic administrative services within the University, aimed at minimising the risks to the health of personnel, faculty members and students. Recent practice has shown that the switch to virtual teaching was quick and effective. It was inclusive, flexible and practical fashioning the maximisation of the use of ICT (information and communication technology) facilities. On the other hand, e-teaching is not being considered as a panacea. It involves important shortcomings, including its negative impact on the social teaching environment that should not be underestimated. For this reason, a wider regulatory framework might be useful involving greater international scholarly cooperation and coordination optimising the supporting and enhancing role of e-teaching to the general traditional education process.

Introduction

The COVID-19 pandemic had a strong transformative impact on higher education at the global level (International Association of Universities 2020). According to a report published by the Organisation for Economic Co-operation and Development (OECD), countries were quick to launch new or to intensify pre-existing virtual teaching methods such as on-line classes or asynchronous teaching programes in order to avoid major disruptions of the teaching process (CEDEFOP. , 2020). In Greece, the pandemic had a transformative effect on the higher education process. The Ministry of Education and Religious Affairs had been quick to respond gradually to the level of emergency as the number of confirmed cases started to increase yet without numbering any deaths. As the entire higher education institutions in Greece, the University of Macedonia in Thessaloniki, had been responsive to the directions provided by both the Hellenic Ministry of Education and Religious Affairs and the Rectors' Council as measures started progressively to be announced.

The unprecedented nature of the health crisis and its progressive evolution leading to a two-months lockdown at the national level generated initial anxiety as regards the fashion with which the educational as well as, research programmes will be implemented. Until then, only specific university courses, including entire courses in the context of the Hellenic Open University or specific vocational training programmes had been using distant learning processes. For instance, they were using particular telecommunication platforms for teaching and teaching material sharing. The University of Macedonia and a great number of its faculty members had a strong experience in supporting courses led by the Hellenic Open University (a public institution) or a large number of other educational or training programmes on the basis of distant learning methods. In this context, the pandemic only intensified a teaching process with which the majority of the faculty members had been familiar. As the number of infected cases started to increase in early February 2020, the University started to respond progressively. The University remained consistent with the general governmental sentiment regarding the need for prompt responses. It was important that decisions had to serve the need to protect the communities' health and ensure that a resilient healthcare system could be able to manage the number of potentially serious incidents. In such an unprecedented health emergency, it was important to establish a virtual working environment for administrative personnel, faculty members and students to continue with their daily tasks from home (BBC, 2020). Certainly, it was a global crisis which started to demonstrate its severity in everyday life without exception, including education. According to reports by UNESCO, almost 1.2 billion of learners were affected and 194 countries closed their educational institutions (UNESCO, 2020). For the purpose of this chapter, analysis will continue with a brief discussion of the way in which Greece and its education authorities responded to the pandemic. It will continue with a discussion on the way in which e-teaching started to be implemented by the University of Macedonia as a general mode of teaching in the midst of lockdown and its aftermath. Finally, it will conclude with an analysis of the advantages and shortcomings stemming from an entire distant learning process.

National Responses to Covid-19 Regarding Higher Education

As shown in diagram 1, the coronavirus outbreak in Greece remained under control, as Athens adopted early on strong measures and thus managed to avoid a disastrous collapse of its public health system.

Diagram 1. Covid-19 Wider Picture in Greece

Countries	**Confirmed Cases**	**Deaths**
Great Britain	364.083	41.703
Spain	566.326	29.747
Germany	258.851	9.347
France	392.243	30.819
Italy	283.180	35.587
Sweden	86.194	5.843

Countries	**Confirmed Cases**	**Deaths**
Albania	10.860	324
Bulgaria	17.598	706
Serbia	32.136	729
Austria	31.827	750
Belgium	90.568	9.917
Israel	147.374	1.086
Greece	12.734	300
As of 13 September, 2020		

Fig. 3, Source: Fotiadi, I. (2020). The Strategy of Tests and Several Centers of Infection, Kathimerini, H ***Στρατηγική των τεστ και οι πολλές «εστίες», 20.***

Due to the high infection rate of Covid-19, as it was bitterly demonstrated in neighbouring Italy at the time, a small number of confirmed cases forced the Greek government to move within a month to a nation-wide lockdown. In fact, initial restriction measures were not considered effective and thus a lockdown was imposed on 23 March 2020. In the meantime, on 10 March 2020, having only 89 confirmed cases and no deaths nation-wide, the Greek government, by entirely endorsing the advice made by the Greek National Public Health Organization, had already decided to suspend the operation of the entire education system, public and private, covering all levels of education including kindergartens (Ministry of Education and Religious Affairs, n.d.). Importantly, as all education institutions suspended their operation, the Ministry wrestled to optimise all previous experiences on distant learning programs (OECD, 2020). In contrast to other levels, for Higher Education the transformation was rather easier. For, during the last several years, universities had become familiar to e-teaching processes, lest in limited extent and certain occasions.

However, the practice of providing distant access to electronic platforms supporting the teaching process to university students and faculty members is widely practiced in Greek universities for a number of years. Nevertheless, the education ministry was quick to launch additional digital tools including a specific web portal in order to provide guidance and information on distant learning and other training programs covering all levels of education. Despite previous experience, the transformation of the entire teaching process through telecommunication instruments and attaining familiarity to various teaching platforms while involving great number of students in the e-classes were not always easy tasks. For Greece, this was an important transformation of the higher education process, which in effect, minimised the missing courses only to laboratory work on certain disciplines, until 25 May 2020, when labs started to work again under safety restrictions (Ministry of Education and Religious Affairs, n.d.). In effect, the entire spring semester of the academic year 2019-2020 was not dramatically affected while exams followed a mixed process of combining oral and interactive exercises through certain electronic platforms. The same process applied to the September re-sit exam period.

In addition, webinars and online thematic conferences accelerated, thus further supporting in an inclusive fashion, the virtual academic process. These initiatives were providing to both speakers and greater audiences a sense of collaboration within the academic community, even if that was taking place in a remote virtual environment (Welle, 2020). As regards the new academic year 2020-21, all education structures apart from the Universities commenced their operation on 14 September 2020, allowing the physical presence of students in classes while adopting particular restrictions protocols and conditions of safety. However, as the rate of confirmed cases have started to grow since the summer months, as seen below, the current picture may change until the end of the year depending on the dynamics of the affected cases.

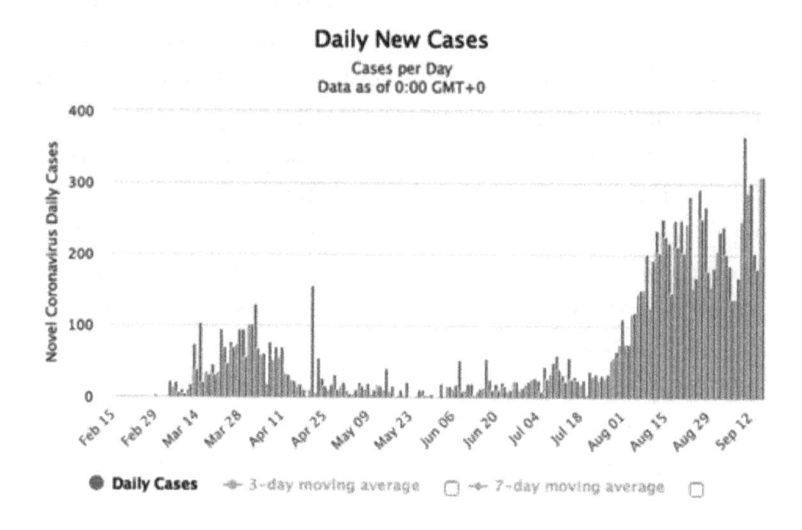

Figure. 4, Source: Worldometer. (2020). Greece Coronavirus Cases: 15,142 Deaths: 338 Recovered: 9,989. https://www.worldometers.info/coronavirus/country/greece/.17 September 2020.

E-teaching Process at the University of Macedonia

The University of Macedonia (UoM) is the second larger institution in the city of Thessaloniki numbering more than 16.000 students and 270 faculty members, researchers and assisting personnel, in its eight departments that also operate 36 postgraduate programmes. In response to directions given by the Greek Ministry of Education and Religious Affairs, UoM started to adjust its practices according to restrictive measures as regards academic mobility and acquired protection material for teachers, personnel and students. On 18 March 2020, the Senate decided to initiate the possibility of distant synchronous (real time) teaching as a process of special circumstances (University of Macedonia, 2020).

By 23 March 2020, real time distant e-teaching commenced progressively to cover both undergraduate and postgraduate classes. By the end of March, the entire teaching courses with the exception of a small number of laboratories at the Department of Music, were conducted virtually (University of Macedonia, 2020). The University further strengthened pre-existing asynchronous teaching platforms to which teaching and research material as well as, curriculum was available to students. An immediate process of transforming textbooks and other related material into electronic material was launched as to make available to all students without exception all related teaching materials.

As regards the teaching process per se, it involved either the use of google meet facility, zoom or other ICT facilities as to activate a virtual e-class procedure following the pre-crisis academic programme. The expediency with which e-teaching was launched and was successfully implemented aimed to avoid the disruption of the spring semester. It was obvious that the health crisis was not about to terminate anytime soon. Therefore, it was important to get prepared as soon as possible as to make the transition from in-person teaching to e-teaching as smooth as possible (Ministry of Education and Religious Affairs. 2020).

For this reason, all distant learning asynchronous platforms the University had been using until then was further enhanced while the Ministry facilitated the establishment of a unified platform for higher education (e-class) which could offer both synchronous and asynchronous teaching and research facilities. Those platforms supported by the existing institutional email network also facilitated the exam processes. As regards the exams, a strict regulation process was initiated according to which students and teachers had to commit themselves as to the preferred exam process. Information about the exact form of the exams, e.g. the use of multiple choice, oral examinations, written assignments, a combination of the two or time limited written exams, was transferred to the university academic authorities.

During the teaching and exam periods the teacher had the ability to interact with the students on several occasions. Importantly, the students were obliged to sign up that plagiarism or other forms of misconduct as regards the use of ICT facilities are not acceptable including the recording of the teaching materials. The exams were either oral through the use of google-meet or an assignment on a topic chosen by the professor or a multiple-choice test during a scheduled timeframe via google docs or questions that should be answered in a paper and sent at a certain time and electronic address. Through PSEPHEDA, the University's Digital Library and Institutional Repository, its members had access to a variety of digital materials, particularly useful for their assignments. In all cases, the protection of personal data was upheld. Students by subscribing via openeclass.com to the courses they preferred to attend, they were able to participate in the online exams and thus complete the semester while being at home. With the use of the University's online platforms, CoMPUs or e-class, students could prepare for classes while library facilities adjusted to distant learning than teaching. Field research was mostly affected because of the mobility and communication restrictions.

In a similar fashion with all other institutions of higher education, UoM proved to be particularly resilient in adjusting to the new situation imposed by Greece's lockdown following the Covid-19 Pandemic. The University was happy to announce that in time frame of few weeks the entire teaching courses had been transformed into virtual e-teaching classes. This was a transformation that demanded extra financial support to empower pre-existing networks and ICT infrastructures as well as, data protection procedures and protocols. This was a process to which attention was given only recently. There have been several issues related to this transformation in teaching that need to be addressed since it touches on both advantages and shortcomings.

Opportunities and Shortcomings of E-teaching

The experience of transforming higher education into a distant e-learning process brings opportunities as well as shortcomings. One positive development out of this emergency process one could see was the inclusive character that the teaching process could take. This is because it facilitates the participation of distant speakers that were not otherwise available. E-teaching evaporates the distance between the teacher and the student and thus invites the organisation of entire teaching programmes without the physical presence. The quick adaptation of people in ICT, means that e-teaching can be proved a useful supporting tool of conventional teaching, especially in cases when education programmes need to attract greater audiences to whom distance used to be the barrier.

The COVID-19 pandemic has forced countries to find effective solutions in order to support children's right to education and allow them to finish their academic year. In this case many modifications have been made in the academic process, which could be adopted even at the post-COVID-19 era. First of all, the digital skills of both students and professors have been improved through the casual use of platforms and more educational materials are available to larger audiences. By the same method, online academic materials have become more accessible to distant audiences. Accordingly, the adoption of distant e-learning courses might be proved a fertile ground as to overcome geographical boundaries and thus, promote cooperation between universities from different countries and continents. It looks more attractive than before for universities to collaborate and thus share e-teaching programs with other universities not available before. Thus, people having minimal opportunities to receive higher education can be benefited by such programmes. Similarly, universities from less advanced countries can be offered such teaching experiences not available before. The availability of academic knowledge through e-teaching to less advanced people is a great promise for the coming decades especially for those people who cannot leave their own city or country to study their preferred discipline (Public Health Update, 2020).

However, there are several drawbacks out of this process. First of all, e-teaching sterilises the teaching from its socialisation process involving the professor and their students. The added value stemming from the personal socialisation through the university environment cannot be replaced by any ICT facility. The oxymoron with e-teaching is that it can be both inclusive as regards participation but utterly impersonal as regards human relations. Thus, personal interaction amongst peers is invaluable for human development and cannot be reduced for long periods to communication through a computer screen.

In sum, asking my students to evaluate the e-teaching courses we conducted all last semester, they had already been tired of the fact that they had to spend more than 10 hours a day in front of a screen and be fully attentive to the discussions, presentations, or seminars. In effect, e teaching can be considered as a supplementary framework to be added in a university curriculum rather than a new teaching framework to replace conventional university teaching. Yet, as an immediate response to an emergency lockdown because of the covid-19 pandemic, e-teaching proved a strong instrument of resilience in the context of higher education.

In addition, other difficulties related to e-teaching regards the availability of the necessary infrastructure as to become operational. These are challenges that need to be overcome. In Greece, one of the most important obstacles regards ICT availability. In particular, although an emergency law was passed by the Greek government, enabling universities to make use of their resources up to 60.000€ without the permission of the Ministry of Finance, in order to procure equipment for distance learning, there are still students that do not own the necessary electronic equipment or the web network as to attend the online courses smoothly. Poor internet connection and technical difficulties due to the high rate of usage are also problems that need to be addressed as they prevent the effective conduct of the online classes and the online exams. In addition, although e-teaching is a more inclusive process, in practice, it excludes students with disabilities. Despite some of the advantages that e-learning offers to them such as avoiding inconvenient travelling, students with visual, sensory or physical limitations might have difficulty in participating in online classes and should thus be provided with special educative material based on their needs (Holloway & Foley, 2018). Another important issue that will attract much attention in the coming years regards the data protection limitations, copyrights of the uploaded research and teaching materials. These are issues that will certainly be discussed in the coming years since e-teaching came and it will remain as a useful mechanism of teaching. Greece is not exception to this process and it might add value to its academic programmes as to attract wider foreign audiences (World Education Blog, 2020).

Conclusion

Covid-19 imposed major transformations in everyday life practices. Education has been one of those practices. As shown in this short analysis, Greece was quick to respond to the issues that Covid-19 was disrupting. As higher education turned digital, resilience was attained. As a specific case, the University of Macedonia in Thessaloniki demonstrated rare flexibility and adaptability as to promptly adjust its academic program to distant synchronous and asynchronous virtual classes. No doubt, even at the time of writing, processes and rules are further adjusted as to address and cover as many challenges as possible in order to attain as safe and democratic teaching as possible while at the same time, be as inclusive as possible especially to the less privileged. E-teaching not only will remain as a practice within universities, but it will be further empowered to evolve hopefully as an instrument of progress rather than exclusion. This points to the question of course, related to the access to high quality of ICT that governments offer to their citizens as to be free to maximise its use for their personal improvement through virtual education.

References

BBC. (2020). "The Covid-19 Changes that Could Last Long-term."

https://www.bbc.com/future/article/20200629-which-lockdown-changes-are-here-to-stay. Accessed on 17 July 2020.

CEDEFOP. (2020). Greece: Responses to the Covid-19 Outbreak, 10 July 2020, https://www.cedefop.europa.eu/el/news-and-press/news/greece-responses-covid-19-outbreak, accessed 30 August 2020).

Holloway, J. & Chris F. (2018). "Pros, Cons for Online Education for Students with Disabilities. https://www.usnews.com/education/online-learning-lessons/articles/2018-05-18/pros-cons-of-online-education-for-students-with-disabilities. Accessed at 17 July 2020.

International Association of Universities. (2020). Covid-19: Higher Education Challenges and Responses. https://www.iau -aiu.net/COVID-19-Higher-Education-challenges-and-responses (accessed 2 September 2020).

Ministry of Education and Religious Affairs. (n.d.) Official Information Website for the Measures Taken from the Greek Government. (http://covid19.gov/category/paideia/). Accessed 30 August 2020.

Ministry of Education and Religious Affairs. (2020). The implementing Distant Education in Higher Education Institutions. (Εφαρμογή της εξ αποστάσεως εκπαίδευσης στα Ανώτατα Εκπαιδευτικά Ιδρύματα», Ελληνική Δημοκρατία Υπουργείο Παιδείας και Θρησκευμάτων), 2020. Εφαρμογή της εξ αποστάσεως εκπαίδευσης στα Ανώτατα Εκπαιδευτικά Ιδρύματα», Ελληνική Δημοκρατία Υπουργείο Παιδείας και Θρησκευμάτων).

https://www.minedu.gov.gr/publications/docs2020/Ex_apostaseos_AEI_16_03_2020.pdf. (Accessed on 17 July 2020.

Ministry of Education and Religious Affairs. (2020). (Διατάξεις Υπουργείου Παιδείας και Θρησκευμάτων», Εφημερίδα της Κυβερνήσεως. https://www.esos.gr/sites/default/files/articles-legacy/pnp_68.pdf . Accessed on 17 July 2020.

Ministry of Education and Religious Affairs. (n.d.). Official webpage of the, Information Regarding the Progressive Relaunch of the Educational Structures. https://www.minedu.gov.gr/koronoios-kentriki

OECD. (2020). Education Responses to Covid-19: Embracing Digital Learning and Online Collaboration. https://www.oecd.org/coronavirus/policy-responses/education-responses-to-covid-19-embracing-digital-learning-and-online-collaboration-d75eb0e8/. Accessed 30 August 2020.

Public Health Update. (2020). "Opportunities and Challenges in Education due to COVID-19.

https://www.publichealthupdate.com/opportunities-and-challenges-in-education-due-to-covid-19/ Accessed on 17 July 2020.

UNESCO. (2020). "Education: From Disruption to Recovery." https://en.unesco.org/covid19/educationresponse. Accessed on 17 July 2020.

University of Macedonia. (2020). Rectors Biannual Review for the Period 1 September 2018 until 31 August 2020. https://www.uom.gr/assets/site/content/adm-68/apologismos-pryt.pdf.

Welle, D. (2020). "How Greece's crisis is helping it bend the COVID-19 curve." https://www.dw.com/en/how-greeces-crisis-is-helping-it-bend-the-covid-19-curve/a-53280532 . Accessed at 17 July 2020.

World Education Blog. (2020). "Covid-19: How is Greece coping with school closure?"

https://gemreportunesco.wordpress.com/2020/04/14/covid-19-how-is-greece-coping-with-school-closure/. Accessed at 17 July 2020.

3

Covid-19 Lockdown Teaching and Learning Responses in Cameroon: Hurdles and Opportunities

Aloysius Nyuymengka Ngalim

Abstract

The study examines and evaluates the various methods implemented by the Cameroon government and other stakeholders since the unprecedented closure of schools and universities due to the COVID-19 outbreak. The shutdown disrupted the teaching and learning of pupils and students, as well as disrupted access for some of the most disadvantaged and marginalised learners. The study argues that evidence on the responses and coping strategies shows that Government has taken measures suggesting that pedagogical approaches to television lectures, digital learning and evaluation should be optimised by using all tools available for pupils and students to continue learning while at home unperturbed. It also contends that the sudden and unplanned shift to the distance mode of teaching is implemented when a large number of teachers have no knowledge of the pedagogy of online teaching and where significant numbers of learners are from deprived areas or homes, out of reach of electricity, technology and internet. Also, the study claims that there is inadequate e-learning infrastructure to support learning and teaching nationwide, and that even the online learning and assessments are untested with a lot of trial and error and uncertainty for everyone. Using the various relevant methods of qualitative research instruments, the study reveals that in spite of efforts to maintain education provision through social media, institutional digital platforms, other distance and online teaching mechanisms, home schooling is not only a massive shock to children's social life and learning pattern but also to parents. However, COVID-19 has exposed the e-learning challenges of Cameroon and provides an excellent opportunity for the country to speed up the building of tech and digital startups as well as, significantly increase access to affordable and reliable high-speed internet in Cameroon's under-served areas. Thus, digital education has a good chance of significant growth during this crisis.

Introduction

Scholarly debates by scientists and medical researchers are abounding on the exact meaning of a pandemic. That is, whether is it a pandemic, or an epidemic? However, the common denominator is that, the term refers to the prevalent occurrence and manifestation of the disease, in excess of what might normally be expected in a geographical region. In the domain of communicable diseases, a pandemic is the worst-case scenario. When an epidemic spread beyond a country's borders, the disease officially becomes a pandemic. Dating from prehistoric to modern times, pandemics and epidemics have atrophied humankind through its existence, often altering the course of history and, at times, signalling the end of entire civilisations. The Black Death (1346-1353) migrated from Asia to Europe, leaving devastation in its wake. Some estimates suggest that it wiped out over half of Europe's population.[1] In 1916 polio epidemics occurred sporadically in the United States, affecting mostly children with 27,000 cases and about 6,000 deaths. From 1918-1920, about 500 million people from the South Seas to the North Pole fell victim to Spanish Flu. It is estimated that about One-fifth of those died (Owen, 2020). The total death toll of the Asian Flu (1957-1958) was more than 1.1 million worldwide, with 116,000 deaths occurring in the United States. The AIDS pandemic and epidemic from 1981 to the present day has exterminated an estimated 35 million lives since it was first identified. The Ebola ravaged West Africa between 2014 and 2016, with 28,600 cases and 11,325 people perished (Owen, 2020). Recently, and beginning in December 2019 a "new" coronavirus began appearing in human beings, in the region of Wuhan, China. It has been named COVID-19, a shortened form of "coronavirus disease of 2019." The COVID-19 pandemic was confirmed to have spread to Cameroon, Central

Africa on 6 March 2020. Since then, the coronavirus has now spread to all 10 regions of the country.

With the coronavirus pandemic, people in Cameroon and the world over have become more aware of the best practices during a pandemic, from careful hand-washing to social and physical distancing. Countries across the world declared mandatory stay-at-home measures, closing schools, businesses, and public places. Dozens of companies and many more independent researchers began working on tests, treatments, and vaccines. This is because the push for the human race to survive the pandemic has become the primary concern in the world. Our focus in this article is on the education sector affected by the sudden outbreak of the pandemic. Thus, the preoccupation is to examine the impact of the COVID-19 on the educational sector in Cameroon and the coping strategies adopted to ensure continuity in teaching and learning after the shutdown of schools and suspension of physical appearance in schools as a measure to prevent the spread of the COVID-19. In other words, examine and evaluate the alternative measures and means to provide students and pupils with lessons while at home.

In these circumstances, it is more insightful to describe Cameroon and the Cameroon educational scene according to the educational traditions in the country before COVID-19 pandemic so that the reader may better appreciate the strategies adopted thus far to assist continuous learning from home.

Background on Cameroon as a Nation

According to the world population review, Cameroon is a culturally diverse coastal country in Africa, which lies on the western side of Africa on the Eastern Atlantic Ocean. Cameroon is bordered by Chad, Nigeria, the Central African Republic, Gabon, Equatorial Guinea, and the Republic of the Congo. The 2018 population is estimated at 24.68 million (World Population View, n.d). This makes Cameroon the 54th most populous country in the world. The country is sparsely populated, however, with just 40 people per square kilometer, which ranks 167th in the world. The urbanisation rate is currently 3.3%; 58% of the country is urbanised and that percentage continues to grow annually. Yaoundé is Cameroon's capital. It was founded in the latter part of the 19th century by German traders during the ivory industry's peak. Yaoundé's population is approximately

2.5 million, which makes it the second-largest city in the country after Douala, which has more than 3 million residents. Douala is said to be the 27th most expensive city on earth, and the most expensive African city (World Population View, n.d.)

Cameroon's economy is based on diversified and self-sufficient agriculture supplemented by substantial petroleum production and a sizable manufacturing sector. Coffee and cocoa are Cameroon's principal agricultural exports, along with cork, wood, and cotton. Agriculture was the main source of growth and foreign exchange until 1978 when oil production replaced it as the cornerstone of growth for the formal economy. The most important cash crops are cocoa, coffee, cotton, bananas, rubber, palm oil and kernels, and peanuts. The main food crops are plantains, cassava, corn, millet, and sugarcane. Palm oil production has shown signs of strength, but the product is not marketed internationally (Encyclopedia.com 2018).

Cameroon is generally referred to as Africa in miniature, given that it possesses a majority of the geographical and cultural characteristics of almost all the regions of Africa (Piot-Lepetite 2017: ix). Cameroon is home of nearly 250 different linguistic groups, even though French and English are official languages. French is spoken by more than 80% of the population in 8 out of the administrative regions of Cameroon. English-speakers of Cameroon (16% of the population in 2015) are located in the Northwest and Southwest regions. Other languages include 55 Afro-Asiatic, 2 Nilo-Saharan, 4 Ubangian, and 168 Niger-Congo Languages (Kouega, 2007).

Cameroon's Educational Sector before COVID-19

Cameroon had and has a public system of schools and universities, but there are also some schools and universities that are run by private investors. Others are run by religious organisations, mainly Christian churches. There are, however, a few Koranic schools. The country has one of the highest school attendance rates in Africa. Most children have access to free, state-run schools or subsidised private and religious facilities (Ebot Ashu, 2016: 20). Since 1990, the number of private institutions has increased dramatically at all levels. The educational system in Cameroon is divided into primary (six years, compulsory), middle school (five years), secondary (high school, two years), and tertiary (University). The Ministries of Education are organised into four divisions, namely: 1) Ministry of Basic Education 2) Ministry of Secondary Education 3) Ministry of technical and vocational division and 4) Ministry of Higher Education. The Ministry of Basic Education is responsible for basic education including pre-schools and primary schools in Cameroon.[2] The Ministry of Secondary Education is responsible for implementing state policies in grammar and technical education. The academic year runs from September to June, end-of-year-examinations are always written exams and the ministry organises at the end of secondary and high school General Certificate of Education Ordinary (GCE) and Advanced Levels examinations respectively in collaboration with the GCE Board. The Ministry of Technical and Vocational Division is in charge of Technical Institutions, vocational and non-formal education. The GCE advanced level and the Baccalaureate (the French equivalent of academic attainment) are the two main entrance qualifications into institutions of higher learning. Finally, the Ministry of Higher Education monitors higher education institutes in Cameroon (Ebot Ashu, 2016: 20-22).

Cameroon is among the African countries south of the Sahara that is making enormous progress in the use of the Information and Communications Technologies (ICTs) in the various development sectors, including education. Private schools introduced ICTs into their curricula in the 1990s though with no specific policy guiding the teaching or use of ICTs in education. ICTs were officially introduced into education in 2001. Since then, the Cyber Education project launched by the Government targets mainly the secondary and tertiary education sectors and to a very lesser extent, the primary sector. The project started slowly, but is now gaining speed with achievements including the establishment of small scale multimedia resources centres (MRCs) in universities, professional/technological schools, and some government secondary schools. The training monitors to manage MRCs, the creation of learning platforms, interconnection of state universities are ongoing projects though too slow for comfort.

However, such projects rely mainly on external funding, thus putting their sustainability into question. Moreover, government secondary schools have poor purchasing power, and no budget has been allotted to them to support ICT-related activities in schools. Most computers used in schools are donations. Private schools have not been involved in the project, thus creating a gap between the two educational systems. Most of the online learning resources accessible through the government secondary school learning platform CAM-EDUC are in French, thus constituting a handicap for the English-speaking community. Moreover, all those online resources are based in Europe, indicating the need for empowering the national stakeholders to enable them to produce online learning materials corresponding to the local environment.

In Cameroon and the wider Africa South of the Sahara, the educational sector is encountering a lot of problems. Harber and Davies (1997) described some of the problems many African countries face in the education industry. According to them, children have few textbooks and other classroom resources, insufficient classroom provisions, inadequate infrastructure, lack of maintenance culture amongst others. Bush and Oduro (2006) explained that in most African countries, the majority of schools in rural areas do not have water, toilets and electricity. Schools often have to function with unqualified or under-qualified teachers. In regard to schooling in Africa, Bush and Oduro (2006) report that most schools in urban areas lack the basic educational resources that can make teaching and learning efficient and constructive. Teachers are paid low salaries, which often results in low morale and motivation, as well as a tendency to seek alternative or additional employment. Typically, teachers do not regard teaching as a successful profession because of less pay scale. The situation affects teaching negatively and has resulted in high levels of unreported absenteeism which, in turn, has negative implications for productivity (Harber and Davies, 1997; Ebot Ashu, 2016:22). In the situation of Cameroon, Tchombe (1997) lays emphasis on the extensive systemic decay, low levels of expenditure on human and material resources, and inadequate focus on leadership development. Despite this situation, more of face-to-face and physical appearance dominated teaching and learning before COVID-19.

Coronavirus in Cameroon

This new Covid-19 virus spreads incredibly quickly among the people in Cameroon. While it was initially seen to be an epidemic in China, the virus spread worldwide within months. The World Health Organization (WHO) declared Covid-19 a pandemic in March 2020, and by the end of that month, the world saw more than a half-million people infected and nearly 30,000 deaths (Staff, n.d).

The COVID-19 pandemic was confirmed to have spread to Cameroon, Central Africa on 6 March 2020 with its first confirmed case (Kouagheu, 2020a). Five new cases were confirmed on 18 March. On 27 March, the total number of COVID-19 cases in Cameroon reached 91. On 30 March, the Minister of Public Health announced that Cameroon had 142 active cases with 6 deaths (Journal du Cameroun, 2020). On 25 April, there were 1,513 confirmed cases of the novel coronavirus in the nation (Aljazeera, 2020). By 5 May, Cameroon had 2,104 confirmed cases and 64 deaths (Kouagheu, 2020b). As of 7 May 2020, there have been over 2,335 confirmed cases of coronavirus disease 2019 (COVID-19), with 111 deaths (fatality rate: 4.1%) (UNICEF, 2020). As of 28 May 2020, there have been over 5,356 confirmed cases, with 177 deaths (fatality rate: 3.3%). In less than three months, the official case tally has risen to nearly 6,600, including 200 deaths. That is, the third-highest number of infections of any country south of the Sahara (Kaze, 2020). Cases have been reported in all ten regions of the country though the majority remains in Central and Littoral regions (UNICEF, 2020).

The Covid-19 situation in Cameroon is rapidly evolving, with dozens of new cases reported each day. In addition to the contemporary challenges linked to conflict and political tensions, the Covid-19 puts Cameroon's education system and economies under amplified pressure. It was in response to the pandemic that the Government of Cameroon implemented since 18 March, 2020, several restrictive and barrier measures among which was the closure of schools and Universities directly affecting the educational lives of about 7.2 million pupils and students across the country, including more than 4.3 million children enrolled in primary schools (Atembeh, 2020). As direct impacts of the pandemic across the nation, all public and private training establishments of various levels of education from nursery schools to higher education, including vocational training centers and professional schools closed up to 2 June 2020 when only national examination preparation classes and universities resumed. In spite of the undesirable impacts, the Government of Cameroon had persistently continued with its relentless efforts to help mitigate the situation as far as the educational sector is concerned especially as pupils and students continue to take preventive measures against COVID-19 by staying at home.

Teaching and Learning during COVID-19 Pandemic

As from 18 March, 2020 all face-to-face meeting and physical appearance was banned in all educational institutions and the preventive quarantine measures implemented. The academic calendar was adjusted; thus, the need to put an update strategy to cope with school closures and ensure classes restarted at a distance emphasising COVID education responses relying on technology. The education ministries announced steps to implement distance learning and assessment during school suspension by putting in place digital learning platforms.

The State launched an e-learning system, especially for families and students with internet access and technology resources. This is because they have access to online platforms especially the WhatsApp, Google classroom and free version of zoom platforms. Educational institutions especially higher education organised tutorials and created video tutorials explaining how to use educational resource websites. Consequently, virtual classrooms were developed and students received codes from their teachers to enter virtual classes to continue electronically. Virtual platforms have been used to organise learning materials, which are gradually enriched over time. Materials in various formats, including videos, were and are being developed by some teacher's proficient with the edtech.

For families without access to internet, the Government designed strategies relying on the use of educational television and radio to broadcast educational programs in order to support learning at home. Thus, the education ministries have been working to ensure that education continuity is implanted in the COVID-19 emergency context, through the national broadcaster, the Cameroon Radio Television (CRTV) as some content offerings have been compiled on the CRTV website. Since 6 April 2020, daily educational programs are broadcasted on CRTV both in English and French to assist learning from home. In other words, the public television station has been offering a special education program for students at all school levels. Every day between 6am and 8pm for pre-school, primary and secondary school children, the program is broadcast. The television broadcasts premiered on the public channels and are also broadcast by private, regional and community channels, with special focus on students expected to take high-stakes national examinations basically on the core subjects.

Problems

Notwithstanding the optimism, e-learning faces numerous pitfalls, remarkably poor internet coverage in many of Cameroon's rural areas as the cost is high beyond their own means. While mobile phones can allow learners to access information and connect with each other and their teachers, most learners live in places not well connected by mobile networks. Limited connectivity and the absence in some rural areas has slowed down the shift to distance learning during COVID-19 and continues to be a major challenge especially in basic education. "A majority of the students do not have access to the internet, especially since many have been asked to return to their homes, often in remote locations," says an academic staff of the University of Bamenda, Cameroon. In other words, relying on connectivity for distance learning achieved very little during school closures. The emergency measures which solely rely on technology are unlikely to offer an adequate response for learning continuity for children at the bottom of the learning pyramid. It is important for the education ministries to implement and continue to implement targeted measures to ensure children from the poorest households can catch up as schools reopen. Too often, school children and students lack the technical means and the funds to follow the courses. These children lose out because of the cost of digital devices and data plans. In some semi-urban and rural towns there is no network and electricity at all. Such infrastructure in some areas where it existed had been damaged by the ongoing Anglophone crisis in some parts of Cameroon.

There exist equity challenges in learning continuity. Studies in low-income settings show lower progression of the most disadvantaged children. The Cameroon government turned to online learning as a handy and effective way to reduce learning loss. This measure did not factor in children from rural areas and disadvantaged schools who hardly would have a computer at home or can carry a cell phone along. Access to internet is even more severely limited and other forms of connectivity are also profoundly un-equal. Very few rural schools have working electricity. In Cameroon, three-quarters of those with cell phones pay through SIM cards and often change service providers and numbers looking for the cheaper provider. Only the privileged households' own radios and televisions to follow lessons. Television, therefore, is yet to be a miracle cure.

One of the major handicaps with learning from CRTV and on-line platforms was and is the unavailability of electricity in most areas together with the phobia Cameroonians have recently developed for the state media. The high frequency of power outages and cuts even in the major cities is another handicap. This means that e-learning has been discriminative in favour of the rich and discriminated between the rural and urban learners.

The teaching of computer sciences in Cameroon is geared more towards acquiring a certificate than considering computer science as a basis for teaching/ learning. In this regard, even computer teachers are not necessarily comfortable with e-learning, a thing that has now forced its way into the Cameroon's school system.

The lack of interactivity between teachers and students is a big minus. Many parents believe that the courses would be more valuable if they were coordinated with the school programme and allowed for teacher-student interaction as is possible with internet teaching. In Buea, Cameroon, a grade four student Carl Nyuymengka, is delighted to be able to "keep in touch with the school" but he is worried about the "lack of interactivity with the teacher, who just does a lecture or corrects homeworks."

The children grumbled of physical and social isolation. "The children are distraught," says Solomon Agbor, father of eight. Most of the kids and younger students interviewed in Buea, the South West Region of Cameroon said, "we were at first happy to sit at home on our computers, tablets and phones all day at the outbreak of COVID-19. It is apparently a reality that devices and technology are merely poor and pitiable substitutes for real social cohesion, interaction, education and network building."

Impact

The impact of COVID-19 has shifted and will seemingly continue to shift Cameroon's educational system in the future. There is a massive widening in the achievement gap. Many students have limited access to the internet where they live. Such a trend could lead a portion of students to fall behind their peers who have greater access to remote learning tools and the time to do assignments.

The COVID-19 pandemic led to the adoption of distance learning by teachers, learners and educational institutions. Many that were once hesitant to offer online lessons have no choice. Teachers were rapidly trained on how to teach online and deploy lessons. It is believed that teachers will continue to update their edtech knowledge while schools update outdated computer equipment and infrastructure as well as, fund professional development training to continue education prior to future crisis.

Parents in Cameroon especially the urban parents that can afford access to internet/television resources and technologies are fast becoming new "substitute teachers" in navigating the school closure period. The parents working from home also play an inordinate part in their children's online learning success. With home lessons, students must first get used to sitting and being at their computers. They must practice discipline. Parents create dedicated learning areas such as desk in their room or a table in the living room as well as, crafting a routine that copycat archetypical school day to encourage children to commit to and continue their distance education. Such functions include the designation of study periods, and recess for students to psychologically and intellectually rejuvenate.

Before examining the way forward, it would be interesting to know the opinion of some academic staff and students on their own experiences of learning and teaching during COVID-19 in Cameroon.

According to Aloysius Ngalim, an Associate Professsor in the University of Buea,

> *I start off my quotidian morning activities during the COVID-19 period by constructing lesson plans which I use a pre-paid web service to upload and assign the lessons to my students in Professional Master's in Library, Archival and Information Sciences. I use video conferencing software to check in with my students especially in a Course like: Preservation and Conservation of Records in Analogue and Electronic Environment. I do same with other courses especially with my PhD students in the Department of History. It's not easy as they are finding it difficult to adapt to the sudden changes and swift shift from physical appearance and face-to-face to integrated digital learning platforms. They are coping as they try to improve as the days go by in spite of challenges such as poor internet or no connectivity and rampant power outages.*

Abit Tracy, a 26-year-old Ph.D student at the University of Buea, Cameroon who lives at Mile 16 says,

The teaching method we use during covid-19 following school closure is the online learning method. This is done through online platforms such as WhatsApp (typing and voice notes), google classroom, and free version of zoom. We also use gmail group (study materials are sent here) as well as emails where we forward assignments. The online teaching and learning methods are good because information is shared without physical contact, thus preventing the spread of coronavirus. To me this learning method is not effective because, there is much laxity on the side of the students. Limited knowledge is impacted during lessons and usually shallow with less depth and breadth. This "forced" online learning has its issues! While learning still goes on, it does not consider the learning or for that matter the teaching styles/personality that takes place in the face-to-face classroom. There are technological options, but they are not the same as the face-to-face and students with dated technology may find it difficult to keep up. Online learning needs hardware and software also. A second-hand desktop, laptop or a good android may be out of the reach of a poor father or mother. Internet connection is another big issue. Broadband and Wi-Fi connection are very expensive and monthly fees may be daunting for the whole family. Another serious problem is rampant electricity cuts. This makes virtual classes impossible.

According to Njodzeka, a 32-year-old Ph.D student in the University of Buea interviewed on the 26 May 2020,

The Coronavirus pandemic and the suddenness with which it affected educational institution unprepared is a call for concern. Schools and Universities have had to respond swiftly in terms of the continuous delivery of teaching and learning. My university, the University of Buea has tried to put in place material and people resources in order to deliver courses that were previously tailored/designed and formulated within a face-to-face format. This means that teachers, lecturers, instructors have had little, if no, time to adapt to the new delivery method coupled with having to learn new skills, competencies and capabilities in order to deliver the 'new normal' of teaching and learning. However, both teachers and students are trying themselves to accustom with online class day by day to continue off-campus classes smoothly. Online classes with teachers who have a good mastery of the various platforms of online teaching are very interesting. In online teaching and learning, teachers who are abroad on mission teach from any part of the world. At first, we missed lectures during such period of teacher's leave of absence. Another advantage of E-learning is the fact that students who miss classes catch up since lectures are recorded. Even in a situation where students don't understand, they can always access the audio or video in their convenience unlike the face-to-face method where lectures are delivered once. Over all, University of Buea has found novel/innovative ways of delivery and the usefulness of latest technologies in facilitation of knowledge building and sharing. It is important to note that online teaching has less sense of teacher control. It is easier for participants to ignore the teacher and social interaction is absent. As good as E learning seems to be, it also has its own challenges. Some of the challenges are poor internet connectivity, chronic power outages and unfamiliarity with online learning/teaching application platforms/technologies by both students and teachers.

In an interview with Enow Marion a Masters student in the University of Buea and a secondary school teacher in Kumba town of the South West Region of Cameroon, her experiences were that,

Technology as a total alternative to the classroom has many limitations. Most are not trained in distance education. In addition, both teachers and students have limitations on technology. Moreover, technical and laboratory-based pedagogy is yet to find a suitable way to continue through online education. In a nutshell, I think that COVID-19 is an opportunity for all actors in the education sector (teachers and students) to use information and communication technologies and tools for education (e-learning). It is true that this teaching method has advantages and disadvantages, but it can be an effective support means for face-to-face teaching. Even teachers can benefit from these tools to facilitate their teaching methods.

The Way Forward/Recommendations

In Cameroon, fewer low-and-lower income-middle-income households have radios, televisions, cell phones and can comfortably access internet as demanded my educational institutions and needs. Given this inequality in connectivity, the gaps between the rich and poor will only continue to heighten in a technologically mediated distance learning environment emphasising learning continuity. There is need for Government to take a pro-poor method. Some of such approaches are:

(a) Government should make available learning materials to families to pick up and perhaps use auxiliary grants by procuring support from development allies to obtain resources for the poorest households. There is also need for the ministry of post and telecommunications and mobile carriers to make available SIM cards, airtime and wifi hotspots for learners at no cost.

(b) Like in Kenya, it is important in Cameroon and even elsewhere to extemporise alternative ways to provide wider internet coverage to the peripheral rural families and students. The Kenyan Civil Aviation Authority (KCAA) in partnership with Alphabet Inc. and Telkom Kenya provided Google's Loon Balloons floating over Kenyan airspace carrying 4G base stations. Loon is a network of stratospheric balloons that provide internet connectivity to rural and remote communities.

(c) Though simple learning activities such as teleteaching, radio, television and SMS messaging could help amplify learning and even maintain engagement in it, they hardly can replace formal curricula. Some Television and Radio stations could focus mainly on e-learning and teaching so that enough time can be allocated for this aspect of education. After all there are channels already allocated only for sports. To mitigate learning loss, the Government should provide low-tech to the poor and disadvantaged households. Also, students without connectivity in the hinterland regions should be able to benefit from the distribution of compiled worksheets.

(d) The teachers and students are in need of incessant training geared towards empowering them with skills related to e-learning for developing and effectively managing online platform learning environments. Thus government and educational institutions should provide training sessions to support teachers and students especially for education in emergency. To swiftly achieve this, ICT should be made compulsory to all the students/pupils in Cameroon. It should also be obligatory for school proprietors to equip computer laboratories with functional and modern computers.

(e) The electricity network should be extended to the rural areas as much as possible and communities should be looking for alternative sources of energy.

(f) Parents should equip their children with minicomputers the same way as mathematical sets, textbooks and calculators.

Conclusion

Most of Cameroon's institutions have been lamentable, with centuries-old, lecture-based approaches to teaching/learning and outmoded classrooms. However, COVID-19 has become a catalyst for educational institutions to search for innovative solutions in a relatively short period of time. Although it is too early to judge how reactions to COVID-19 will affect the education system in Cameroon, there are signs suggesting that it could have a lasting impact on the trajectory of learning innovation and digitisation. As the COVID-19 pandemic runs its course, it is apparently a quintessential adaptive and transformative challenge as a design process and implementation of adaptive responses to the emerging challenges were crafted. As earlier revealed, the comprehensive outcome of the Covid-19 pandemic is difficult to predict, at the time of this writing. But we can learn from pandemics in history to determine our best courses. These are our teachers – the Spanish flu, the AIDS pandemic, and more. From field evidence, it is clear that most COVID-19 responses in education will end up by privileging better-of-children. Students with greater levels of connectivity, higher levels of parental education, greater availability of parental time for engagement, and in-home availability of books and materials have much better ability to access and benefit from distance learning. However, it is unlikely that the above recipe of interventions will be able to wholly mitigate against scholarship loss, especially for the poor households. Thus, there is need for Government to plan remedial strategies and methods to ensure that children of deprived households can return to school and catch up with their peers when schools resume.

Schools in Cameroon resumed 2 June, 2020 and again only for qualifying examination levels (class six, form five, upper sixth and the higher education sector. The rest of the other levels have continued with online classes. Online learning has come to stay. The education ministries and institutions need to empower both the teachers and the students to be abreast with the new form of learning and teaching for a "new virtual Cameroon" to be reborn as digital education has a good chance of significant growth during this crisis. It is hoped that such innovations will provide an opportunity for the scholastic institutions to move a step further to the third-generation model of education.

Endnotes

1. It was caused by a strain of the bacterium *Yersinia pestis* spread by fleas on infected rodents. The bodies of victims were buried in mass graves. See Owen Jarus. 20 of the Worst Epidemics and Pandemics in History. https://www.livescience.com/worst-epidemics-and-pandemics-in-history.html Accessed 19 May 2020.

2. At the end of every academic school year this ministry organises three examinations for primary six pupils, that is First School Living Certificate (FSLC), the Common Entrance (CE), and the Technical Entrance examination.

References

Agence France-Presse. (2020). With Virus Lockdowns, Africa Gears Up for Remote Schooling. https://www.journalducameroun.com/en/with-virus-lockdowns-africa-gears-up-for-remote-schooling/ Accessed 23 March 2020.

Aljazeera. (2020). "Coronavirus: Which Countries have Confirmed Cases?" 25 April 2020. Accessed 25 April 2020.

Atembeh L. (2020). "The impact of Covid- 19 on Education in Cameroon." https://www.greenvision.news/the-impact-of-covid-19-on-educational-in-cameroon/. Accessed 1 June 2020.

Bush, T. and Oduro, G. (2006) New principals in Africa: preparation, induction and practice. Journal of Educational Administration, 44 (4), 359-375.

Ebot A. F. (2014) Effectiveness of School Leadership and Management Development in Cameroon. A Guide for Educational Systems, Schools, and School Leaders. Newcastle Upon Tyne: Cambridge Scholars Publishing.

Ebot A. F. (2016). "History as It Relates to Educaitonal Leaership and Management of Education in Cameroon." *Educational Leadership and Management Studies*. Volume 35 No 2.

Encyclopedia.com. (2018). Cameroon." Worldmark Encyclopedia of Nations. http://www.encyclopedia.com/history/encyclopedias-almanacs-transcripts-and-maps/cameroon-0. Accessed 1 June 2020

Harber, C. and Davies, L. (1997). School Management and Effectiveness in Developing Countries. London: Cassell.

Kaze, R. (2020). Cameroon Government Under Fire as Virus Tally Rises. https://www.barrons.com/news/cameroon-government-under-fire-as-virus-tally-rises-01591268709. 4 June 2020.

Kouagheu, J. (2020a). "Cameroon Confirms First Case of Coronavirus". *Reuters.* https://www.reuters.com/article/us-health-coronavirus-cameroon-idUSKBN20T10Z Accessed 6 March 2020.

Kouagheu, J. (2020b) "Au Cameroun, sur la Piste du Coronavirus dans les Quartiers de Douala". Accessed 5 May 2020.

Kouega, J.P (2007). "The Language Situation in Cameroon." *Current Issues in Language Planning.* 8 (1), 3-94.

Owen Jarus. (2020). 20 of the Worst Epidemics and Pandemics in History. https://www.livescience.com/worst-epidemics-and-pandemics-in-history.html Accessed 19 May 2020.

Piot I. (2017). Cameroon in the 21st Century: Challenges and Prospects. Volume 2. New York: Nova Science Publishers, Inc.

Staff. "Outbreak: 10 of the Worst Pandemics in History." https://www.mphonline.org/worst-pandemics-in-history/

Tchombe, T. (1997) Structural Reforms in Education in Cameroon. Yaoundé: Cameroon. Available from: http://www.educationdev.net/educationdev/Docs/Cameroon.PDF. Accessed December 2010.

UNICEF. (n.d). Cameroon: COVID-19 Situation Report #09 (May 1st - 7th). https://reliefweb.int/report/cameroon/cameroon-covid-19-situation-report-09-may-1st-7th. Accessed 1 June 2020.

UNICEF. (n.d.) Cameroon: COVID-19 Situation Report #11 (May 15 – May 28). https://reliefweb.int/report/cameroon/cameroon-covid-19-situation-report-11-may-15-may-28. Accessed 1 June 2020.

World Population View. (n.d). http://worldpopulationreview.com/countries/cameroon-population/. Accessed 16 April 2018.

Section II

Societal Effect and Schooling During Pandemic

4

COVID-19 Pandemic and its Impact on Canadian Society and on Teaching and Learning

Nivedita Das Kundu

Abstract

The outbreak and lockdown due to COVID-19 pandemic has disrupted social life and education system in Canada like many other countries in the world. The chapter tried to examine how rapid spread of COVID-19 affected country's health care sector and due to lockdown and closing of many industries, commercial establishments, retails and educational institutions, Canada's economy got badly affected. Due to COVID-19, all the educational institutions in Canada were forced to close till end of Summer. The chapter argued that everyone in Canada is trying to adapt to the new reality. The chapter broadly analyses that though online teaching and learning continued and will continue for some more time along with few in-person visits to schools, it is evident that online education cannot fully replace the in-class experience. But the goal is to help students to continue their education and the learning process. There have been challenges adjusting to these changes for students and for both parents and teachers. It is hoped that this phase of a tough time will end soon and COVID-19 vaccine will be introduced by the end of 2020 to bring back normalcy in everyone's life. The chapter attempts to focus that COVID-19 has taught everybody to increase patience, resilience, adaptability and how to overcome any such future challenges and hardship.

Introduction

The outbreak of the COVID-19 Pandemic in Canada from the middle of March 2020 affected the Canadian population with unexpected disruptions in almost all spheres of life. The pandemic drastically altered the lifestyle in most of the provinces in Canada. Prime Minister Justin Trudeau requested Canadians to stay at home and self-isolate. Each province in Canada implemented its measures and plans to fight COVID-19. The provinces like British Columbia, Saskatchewan, Manitoba, Ontario, New Brunswick, Nova Scotia and Prince Edward Island declared a state of emergency. Alberta, Northwest Territories, Quebec, Newfoundland & Labrador have issued public health emergencies. Similar warnings have been applied at the municipal levels as well. Most of the Canadians trust their government institutions. Hence, people tried to obey government advisories and tried to follow the instructions given by government bodies to ensure that the health-care system can work properly and does not become overwhelmed. However, the disruptions in normal life became evident as state borders and borders with United States of America were shut down, supply chains were broken, consumer demand collapsed, educational institutions were closed. That is, almost all the entire sectors of the economy closed. Canadians became worried about paying for their groceries and their bills. The situation became especially grim for a vulnerable population especially the homeless who were not able to self-isolate themselves and avoid getting affected by the pandemic.

The rapid spread of the coronavirus in Canada demonstrated how much interconnected the global systems have become. This pandemic made Canadians change their daily routine. It seems, in a short period the threat of COVID-19 became more dangerous. The COVID-19 virus killed a huge number of people in a few weeks' time and long term care facilities and retirement homes got badly affected due to COVID-19. Unfortunately, in Canada around 80 percent of all COVID-19 deaths were in the senior homes (Grant, 2020). The analyses made in this chapter is based on both the primary and secondary source information. The chapter argued that the effects of the COVID-19 virus rippled through the Canadian system and the crisis has dented many. The chapter tried to examine how COVID-19 pandemic deepened the crisis in the education, economic and health care sector. The chapter also attempted to focus on how COVID-19 pandemic has pushed the innumerable population into poverty to meet their demands as many faced difficulties in storing food in their refrigerators. The chapter also touched upon the fact that responses of the community helped to protect vulnerable populations and financial support by the federal and provincial governments helped the population of Canada to certain extend in COVID-19 difficult time.

Brief Background

The science suggests that this virus came from bats and likely to have made a jump from bats to humans sometime in late 2019, in China's Wuhan city. This virus has an incredible ability to spread among people who are close to each other, not wearing masks. Because of worldwide travel, this virus infected people and the infection went all over the world as borders to travellers were not closed for a long time. Thus, the virus continued to spread fast and gradually, it has taken over the Canadian cities in a short period of time. Things started to change for the worse during the month of March, as cases started to rise rapidly across the country. The fight against COVID-19 became a massive effort for Canadian health care sector. Canada announced a lockdown from the middle of March 2020. Closure of all commercial and retail businesses was announced. All schools, colleges and universities were closed, except for essential services like healthcare, banks, security facilities and groceries. The state borders were sealed and the government banned all non-essential travels, except in cases of inevitability.

Pandemic Support

The federal government declared to provide economic assistance in various ways. The low or zero interest business loans were announced, tax payment deferrals were declared, payroll tax holidays were given and there was expanded access to employment insurance (EI). The government also boosted the Canada Child Benefit (CCB) and the goods and service taxes (GST) rebates. Plans were announced to ensure bank liquidity along with various stimulus spending proposals. Working-age people who relied on employment or self-employment as their primary source of income were badly affected by widespread business closures. Many who fall in the lower end of the income distribution were severely impacted. Looking into these difficulties, the federal government implemented the provision of a monthly income of Canadian Dollar (CAD) 1,000 to all individual working-age Canadians who had employment or self-employment income in 2019.

The federal government also announced the "Canada Emergency Students Benefit." Students were significantly concerned about paying their tuition fees and also concerned about paying back their student loans. They were worried about paying for their regular expenses due to the loss of part-time jobs. The Canadian Prime Minister Justin Trudeau also announced that people who qualify for old age security would be eligible for a one-time, tax-free payment of CAD 300 to help offset increased costs due to the pandemic and that people eligible for the Guaranteed Income Supplement (GIS) will get an extra CAD 200 (Government of Canada, 2020).

While Canada has been able to manage the coronavirus crisis so far, Canada's ability to continue to keep people safe from the pandemic and at the same time successfully rescue the economy will be quite difficult looking into the present situation. This pandemic has made one thing clear that no one is safe unless the whole community is safe and maintains safety. Many started re-thinking about the idea of globalisation and today many think it might have lost its significance and started favouring the idea of local self-sufficiency.

Teaching and Learning during Pandemic

Due to the COVID-19 pandemic, the year 2020 has been tough for Canada's young population. In Canada, digitisation became a reality and within a few weeks of the lockdown digital cafes, Google meet-ups, zoom meetings and other virtual remote work arrangements enabled Canadians to continue with their work and educational activities from home. COVID-19 disrupted the Canadian educational system in schools, colleges and universities. All the institutions were closed following the March break and it was expected that the online education will continue for a few months. Today, everyone in Canada is trying to adapt to the online education system. Though online learning cannot fully replace the in-class experience, the main aim is to help students to continue their education and the learning process. There have been challenges adjusting to these changes for both students and teachers. Educators and officials continuously tried to deliver messages of positivity and ensure that equity should be maintained during the online education. There were both live and pre-recorded lessons delivered online. For the special needs students, the online classes were and are tough to adjust. However, the teachers are supporting these students through online meetings and with extra consultations. Teachers also addressed the digital deficiencies of parents of young students struggling to learn how to navigate the online tools and assist their children.

Every academic institution before starting the online classes crafted a plan to address the needs of students who may not have access to the internet, computers or tablets. The Ministry of Education collaborated with tech-companies to provide technological support for the 'learn at home', programs to help meet the educational needs of students and teachers. Devices were distributed to students who didn't have them along with a fast internet facility. Educational institutions provided these facilities at no cost and will continue to provide the facilities until the situation improves. During the online teaching, students and teachers have been maintaining continuous communication with one another, especially, through email or video communications. However, in these digital days, students being stuck at home during lockdown also increased uninterrupted access to television (TV) and social media, which is causing a negative impact in many school and college-going students and affecting their mental health. Results from a recent rapid assessment study conducted to assess the impact of COVID-19 on young people in Canada showed that adolescents who are active social media users reported to be spending more time online during the lockdown. Many adolescents reported feeling depressed and are said to have been watching more TV during the lockdown (Schaefer and Wasyliw, 2019). The shutting down of educational institutions has made life difficult for the adolescents and more challenging. While digital literacy will undoubtedly be the new normal in the post-COVID-19 era, it is equally important to assess the holistic impact of the pandemic on adolescent health, development and well-being. Inclusive learning solutions are critical to addressing the needs of the most vulnerable and marginalised children to bridge the digital divides in society. Nonetheless, the self-isolation regime allowed some students to concentrate more on their studies as other activities became limited. Students were communicating with their friends and classmates through FaceTime, what's app and they became used to this medium of communication. During the time of pandemic, people became more considerate and understanding regarding expectations from both teachers and students.

It is hoped that the phase of lockdown time provided the young population of Canada with the opportunity to practice and learn adaptability, patience, resilience to overcome any such challenges and hardships in future too. Albeit it might be difficult to understand whether hard immunity is beginning to form in Canada with its young and healthy population anchoring the shield for the community. However, it seems the second wave started when full-fledged schools, transportation movement and economic activity gradually returned. The challenge will be to augment the public health infrastructure and precautionary protocols in a manner that will enable Canadian society to effectively tackle future waves. Back-to-School started in Canada in September and additional federal investments and resources to support the return to class in the fall has been implemented. Provincial and federal governments are both spending money towards personal protective equipment (PPE), on enhanced cleaning of the schools and buses, on improving ventilation, and hiring more cleaning and teaching staff. Provincial and federal governments are also adopting additional public health protocols for all the schools, such as the hiring of up to 500 public health nurses. An aggressive mandatory masking policy for grades 4-12 has been introduced, and a surveillance testing strategy for secondary school students have also been introduced to ensure a successful return to the classrooms and to prevent and minimise COVID-19 outbreaks in the schools and keep all the students safe (Peel District School Board, 2020).

A protocol has been developed to deal with students who become sick while at school, including isolation, and providing PPE to the sick student and staff. Parents are being asked to screen their children every day before school, and to keep them home if they are sick. If someone in a school, be it a student or staff member, tests positive for COVID-19, the school community will take care of that. Immediate and rigorous contact tracing is done regularly. (Peel District School Board, 2020). The school will close down if public health officials determine it is not safe for students and staff.

The government, led by Public Health Ontario, intends to carry an asymptomatic surveillance test on secondary school students in Canada. On top of having public health nurses in every school, education staff had to undergo complete rigorous professional development on health and safety. The local government is implementing extra health and safety measures and are investing adequate money for that. Also, the local government is taking care of the safety, protection, and well-being of Ontario's students. Apart from the initiatives of the federal and provincial government, everybody is trying to do their part, and it is truly remarkable to see the work that can be accomplished. Government of Canada has also increased investments in mental health, because everyone understands how difficult this period has been for every family. During pandemic time every school in Canada will continue to practice inclusion, compassion and optimism in the hearts and minds of all the students and teachers.

Pandemic Travel Restriction

In Canada, the restrictions on international and domestic travel continued due to the pandemic and because of that people started noticing clear skies and the pollution level decreased drastically probably not seen in decades. Due to the complete travel stoppage, very few aeroplanes could be spotted crossing the sky, which is extremely rare in the bigger cities in Canada. Also, it is rare to see major streets empty as everybody was asked by the provincial and federal government to mostly stay at home and maintain distance. People of Canada obeyed the restrictions during the lockdown period and stayed at home in the hope that everything will become normal within a few weeks. People started cooking for themselves at home, entertaining themselves within their home, as no activities were allowed outdoor. The professional sports, theatres, restaurants, clubs and bars all were closed to avoid the spread of the virus. This pandemic helped Canadians to be more connected with their local community and local system. However, gradually the lockdown eased with the restrictions and all the business activities started opening up in phases, but in the second wave, once again certain restrictions were imposed in hot spot- red zone areas.

Travel restrictions also affected Migrant labourers, especially those who came from various places for seasonal work. Migrant labourers come for work in the agricultural sector, service sector and also in physically demanding labour at construction sites and factories. They all suffered due to COVID-19 travel restrictions, as borders were closed and lockdown implemented. Canadian agricultural sector is highly dependent on migrant workers. Thousands of migrant work forces got affected they were stopped from entering Canada. This decision affected the food supply chains. In order to reduce the difficulty in certain seasonal agricultural sectors, college and university students were recruited but such options could not work in all the sectors as many sectors required skilled and dedicated workers which were difficult to get during the pandemic time. Many international students faced problems during pandemic time to get back to their home country due to travel restrictions. Also, many new students who were supposed to come to join the fall semester in September could not attend school/colleges/universities due to travel restrictions and lack of flights.

Pandemic Treatment

Canada is a diverse country with many languages, religious beliefs, ethnicity, culture, and lifestyle. Canada's geography and diversity of populations created challenges in delivering health care during the pandemic. Community size and accompanying health care resources vary significantly across the country. During the COVID-19 pandemic in Canada, family physicians, nurses, practitioners, pharmacists provided assessment and treatment for the COVID-19 patients. Local hospitals were responsible for providing treatment for more seriously ill patients with COVID-19 symptoms. Emergency departments and intensive care units in every hospital were given special attention. Many patients in remote and isolated communities were transferred to larger centres, based on initial and secondary assessment. Mental health services, social services and other community support services also helped in supporting the sick and vulnerable population (Government of Canada, 2020). Telemedicine also provided useful support to many communities in remote places and in places with harsh weather conditions.

The COVID-19 pandemic has created an unprecedented demand for Canada's health care system and has led to an urgent need for access to health products. These measures are helping to make health products needed for COVID-19, such as investigational drugs and vaccines available to Canadians health care workers. Canada is also working with international partners on a coordinated and well-aligned approach during the pandemic. This ensures that Canada's policies and regulatory approaches are aligned and that health products are safe, effective and quickly available to the Canadians (Government of Canada, 2020). Collaboration also helps advance the development of diagnostics and treatments that could save lives and protect the health and safety of people everywhere in the country. Drugs including vaccines are regulated under the "Food and Drugs Act and Regulations", of Canada. They must meet the regulatory requirements for safety, efficacy and quality before they can be sold in Canada. On 27th July 2020, Health Canada granted authorisation with conditions for the use of Veklury (remdesivir) to treat COVID-19 in patients with pneumonia requiring supplemental oxygen. Remdesivir is the first drug to be authorised in Canada for the treatment of COVID-19 (Government of Canada, 2020).

In all likelihood, this pandemic will stay for long until a vaccine is invented. Currently, there are no vaccines authorised for COVID-19 treatment in Canada. A Chinese and Canadian research team has been conducting clinical trials on a COVID-19 vaccine. China has asked to test the vaccine in Canada. The National Research Council is also scaling up its vaccine production capacity in anticipation that Health Canada will approve the trial. On 13th May, Health Canada released a statement mentioning that blood tests, known as serological tests, will be used in Canadian laboratories to detect antibodies specific to COVID-19 (Health Canada, 2020). There are many potential drugs being tested in Canada for use against COVID-19. Canada is closely tracking all potential drugs and vaccines. Potential COVID-19 drugs currently being tested in Canadian clinical trials are antiviral drugs, anti-malarial drugs, monoclonal antibodies and other drugs that address inflammation, convalescent plasma collected from patients who have recovered from COVID-19 (Health Canada, 2020).

Health Canada is presently reviewing scientific evidence of a drug or vaccine, including results from clinical trials, to assess the product's safety, efficacy and quality before it can be sold in Canada. To facilitate earlier access to COVID-19 drugs or vaccines, health Canada, is prioritising the review of these products while ensuring there is adequate evidence of safety, efficacy and quality to merit access to Canadians. Health Canada is also collaborating with international counterparts and leveraging all available knowledge to the extent possible to support and expedite the authorisation of drugs for COVID-19 in Canada (Government of Canada, 2020). Domestically, health Canada is actively engaging with the industry associations and specific drug sponsors to learn as much as possible about potential therapies and facilitate their availability in Canada.

Conclusion

The COVID-19 pandemic time, the lockdown measures and self-isolation have changed many things around the world and the same happened in Canada as well. People were forced to spend more time in the virtual world. However, during the pandemic, people with other diseases began to suffer as Canadian health care sectors were focused more on COVID-19 patients. Until recently, Canadian Senior homes could not think that the senior support system in Canada may not be able to cope-up with the challenges of the pandemic and refused to accept the threat of this new pandemic as a reality. Similar to many other nations in the world, the COVID-19 pandemic and the massive influx of senior patients support system in senior care homes became insufficient in Canada. The consequence is that senior homes and Canadian seniors suffered the most.

The COVID-19 pandemic has taught Canadians that there is a need to change their lifestyle, control excessive urbanisation, reduce excessive mobility and protect the environment. During the management of the COVID-19 pandemic, many things came forward. For instance, the reality of global governance became prominent at the same time and political fragmentation also increased during the pandemic time.

Perhaps, now it is also the time to empower international institutions to establish the rule of law globally. Today, international institutions have entered a phase of lack of significance. In the case of COVID-19, it is believed that the World Health Organisation (WHO) did not play the responsible role that it should have played. The WHO declared too late to the world about COVID-19 as a "pandemic." The delaying reduced the ability of many countries to react on time.

The COVID-19 pandemic has taught Canadians that access to health care, medication, housing, and basic income for all is the most essential for the citizens. Now it is the time to fundamentally restructure the societies around the ideals of local self-sufficiency and environmental sustainability. Perhaps, now it is also the time to empower international institutions to establish the rule of law globally. More, for decades, it has been believed that the best institution to guarantee people's security and safety is the military institutions. It was believed that the main threat to citizen's security emanates from other states aggressiveness. To protect citizens from these threats, all states must maintain powerful military institutions of their own in order to assure peace and safety as well as protect the Nation and its people. This mentality seemingly changed during this pandemic that posed threats to human security and peace more than any other thing mankind has ever experienced. Viruses like COVID-19, SARS, Spanish flu, threatens human health security directly and pushes a countless number of the population into extreme poverty and causes severe environmental destruction. The larger lesson taught during this pandemic is that there is a need to allocate a large budget for the health care sectors and maintain good health care facilities. The federal government ought to inject more funds for improving medical needs, invest in health care research, focus on increasing medical supplies, and provide support to health care personnel.

During the pandemic time Canadian government tried their best to protect the teaching and learning process, to ensure that the education is reached to a significant number of students in order to continue learning even in the difficult pandemic period. Though COVID-19 pandemic is creating challenges in the teaching and learning process, but it also initiated reforms in the education system for better and increased the use of technology. In many educational institutions, the move to e-learning became an opportunity to expand flexible learning modalities, setting the stage for a sustained shift towards more online learning and move towards digitisation. The Canadian government also used different strategies and methods to facilitate the entire student's community to take care of their education as well as, mental and physical health issues and concerns. The inclusive learning process was encouraged so that vulnerable and marginalised societies should not get affected. It is hoped that this phase of a tough time will provide everyone with the opportunity to practice and learn to adjust, to be more tolerant, to be more flexible and be able to overcome any such future difficulties and situations.

References

Grant, K. (2020). 81% of COVID-19 deaths in Canada were in long-term care – nearly double OECD average. https://www.theglobeandmail.com/canada/article-new-data-show-canada-ranks-among-worlds-worst-for-ltc-deaths/. Accessed on March 2020.

Government of Canada. (2020). Coronavirus Disease (COVID-19): For Health Professionals. https://www.canada.ca/en/public-health/services/diseases/2019-novel-coronavirus-infection.html. Accessed on April 2020.

Schaefer, L and , Wasyliw, D. (2019). What is the impact of physical education on students' well-being and academic success? https://www.edcan.ca/articles/impact-physical-education-students-well-academic-success/?gclid. Accessed on May 2020.

Peel District School Board. (2020)a. Reopening Plans 2020-21 School Year. https://www.peelschools.org/schools/reopening/Pages/default.aspx. Accessed on August 2020.

Peel District School Board. (2020)b. Enhanced Health and Safety Measures. https://www.peelschools.org/schools/reopening/Pages/default.aspx. Accessed on August 2020.

Government of Canada. (2020). COVID-19 pandemic guidance for the health care sector .https://www.canada.ca/en/public-health/services/diseases/2019-novel-coronavirus-infection/health-professionals/covid-19-pandemic-guidance-health-care-sector.html. Accessed on August 2020.

Government of Canada. (2020). Guidance Document: Notice of Compliance with Conditions (NOC/c). https://www.canada.ca/en/health-canada/services/drugs-health-products/drug-products/applications-submissions/guidance-documents/notice-compliance-conditions.html. Accessed on May 2020.

Health Canada. (2020). Statement from Health Canada on COVID-19 Serological Tests. https://www.canada.ca/en/health-canada/news/2020/05/statement-from-health-canada-on-covid-19-serological-tests.html. Accessed August 2020.

Government of Canada. (2020). Drugs and vaccines for COVID-19. https://www.canada.ca/en/health-canada/services/drugs-health-products/covid19-clinical-trials.html. Accessed on August 2020.

5

The Covid-19 Pandemic Lockdown and the Paradigm Shift in Lecture Delivery Methods in Cameroon Universities: Problems and Prospects

Brenda Nachuah Lawyer & Emmanuel Shu Ngwa

Abstract

History has recorded that between 2019 and 2020, humanity was entangled in a global health pandemic – the outbreak and wide human-to-human spread of a deadly 2019 strain of the Corona Virus Disease (COVID-19). The massive spread of this disease and the resultant high fatality rates from Asia, through Europe, America and to Africa, led to a complete lockdown of human socio-economic and political activities and interactions by world governments in March 2020, as one of the major containment strategies. The Republic of Cameroon was therefore not left out. However, mindful of the critical importance of higher education to societal and sustainable development; the survival of teaching-learning activities within university circles during the COVID-19 pandemic lockdown could only have been through a paradigm shift in traditional lecture delivery methods in order to meet up with the existing reality and ensure continuity. Though living in an era of Information Communication Technologies (ICTs), the traditional form of teaching in Cameroon Universities, like in most Sub-Saharan African Universities, has often involved face-to-face lectures to large groups of students, accompanied by tutorials and workshops, with some independent study. But, the COVID-19 lockdown resulted in a radical change, as university administrations, staff and students were forced to fully embraced e-learning (online teaching-learning) and blended learning approaches under the general supervision of the Ministry of Higher Education. What were the stakes involved in this radical change? What was problematic in its implementation and what does the future holds for such emergency interventions in the higher education sector of the country? Anchored on the theoretical frames of Education in Emergencies (EiE), and the Culturo-Techno-Contextual-Approach model; this chapter examines the COVID-19 pandemic lockdown and paradigm shift in lecture delivery methods in Cameroon Universities. After analyzing the E-learning and blended learning methods generally adopted by the universities, and the problems encountered, the authors projected strong stakeholders-collaboration in the building of quality e-learning infrastructures in the country and adequate staff and student capacities on online teaching-learning innovations. Such measures would not only ensure a high quality and sustainable blended teaching-learning system within the country's universities in an era of ICTs, but would most importantly prepare these institutions for easy adaptation in teaching-learning during future lockdowns or emergencies like the COVID-19.

Introduction

According to the World Health Organization (WHO) (2020), the infectious Coronavirus disease 2019 (COVID-19) is caused by severe acute respiratory syndrome coronavirus 2 (SARS-CoV-2). The virus is mostly transmitted through droplets generated when an infected person coughs, sneezes, or exhales. The virus that originated from Wuhan, China in late 2019 was declared a Public Health Emergency of International Concern (PHEIC) in January 2020, as it progressively spread across the world resulting to high fatality rates in Asia, Europe and America (WHO, 2020).

In March 2020, the spread of COVID-19 was already at its peak, with cases recorded in the African continent. Alarmed by the spread and severity of the virus, WHO, after an assessment decided to declare it a global pandemic on 11th March, 2020. The most intense amongst several measures recommended by WHO and other international health stakeholders to contain the spread of COVID-19 was a global lockdown in March 2020. All socio-economic, political, and cultural activities were strictly limited and, in some cases completely shut down. Human interaction from Asia, Australia through Europe, Americas, and Africa was therefore grounded, as people confined themselves as an emergency safety measure against the uncontrollable spread of the deadly virus. Though Africa was not extremely hit by the COVID-19 pandemic as compared to the rest of the world, Cameroon was however amongst the most affected countries in Africa south of the Sahara. The rapid spread of the pandemic in the country, therefore, justify the 13 measures taken by the Cameroon government to contain the spread of the virus in the country which included a complete shutdown of all educational institutions from basic to tertiary levels, including vocational training centres and professional schools and the indefinite postponement of the annual University Games for 2020 (Sunjo, Wuyt and Saidu, 2020).

In the face of this pandemic and health emergency, coupled with the resultant lockdown, the education system and particularly higher education which is a key determinant of knowledge-based economies (OECD, 2009) and sustainable development in any nation (Longshurt, 2014) was at stake. There was need to sustain teaching-learning in these institutions across Africa and specifically in Cameroon which had hitherto been done largely through face-to-face teaching. It was, therefore, important to guarantee continuity in knowledge acquisition, capacity building and sustainable economic development through teaching, research and other educational services during and after the pandemic lockdown. Such guarantees could only have been put in place through a paradigm shift in the lecture delivery methods that had been in use in tertiary institutions of learning prior to the outbreak of the COVID 19 pandemic and the subsequent lockdown. New Era (2020) corroborated this by challenging higher education institutions to adopt innovative solutions and transition to a new normal amidst the current COVID-19 crisis. Consequently, this chapter examined the COVID-19 pandemic lockdown and the paradigm shift in lecture delivery methods in Cameroon Universities.

Theoretical and Legal Framework

This paper is theoretically underpinned by the theory of Education in Emergency propounded by UNESCO (2019) and the Culturo-Techno-Contextual (CTC) Approach model by Okebukola (2019).

1. Education in Emergency

This refers to a crisis situation created either by a conflict, disaster or pandemic which destabilizes, disorganizes or destroys the structured education system, and so requires an integrated process of crisis and post-crisis response (UNESCO, 2019). According to UNHCR (2019), emergencies are natural disasters such as floods and earthquakes, and man-made crises such as civil strife and war as well as health emergencies such as HIV/AIDS, Ebola and Cholera amongst others. It could also be conflict such as political crises. Even though the provision of education in every nation is primarily the responsibility of the state, it is however the responsibility of all stakeholders especially during such emergencies. Some of these stakeholders include parents, individuals, community-based organizations, the United Nations, national/international governmental and non-governmental organizations. Consequently, in terms of policy, educational emergency derives its roots from the right to education, acknowledged in international humanitarian laws and statutes. The resolution which was unanimously approved by the 192 Member States of the UN reaffirms the importance of education in an emergency by setting it as a right for every human being.

The COVID-19 pandemic and the global lockdown was a clear case of an emergency. The declaration of the disease by WHO as a global pandemic meant that it had become a health emergency. Hence, it not only required swift responses with measures to contain the widespread of the deadly virus, but also emergency education measures to sustain the higher education sector which is a critical preparative agent for post-pandemic recovery. It was a critical emergency where nations and global economies were in a complete lockdown and economies in crises. Education, however, remained at the top of the priority list of the Cameroon nation and individual families. This was justified by the efforts and measures taken by the Cameroon government to guarantee continuous teaching and learning during the lockdown. It, therefore, ought to be the responsibility of the Cameroon government, UNESCO and all other education stakeholders in the country to work in collaboration to help strengthen the education sector to ensure that life-saving information, knowledge, skills and researches continued flowing from the country's higher institutions of learning to the citizens.

2. Culturo-Techno-Contextual Approach (CTCA) Model

The Culturo-Techno-Contextual (CTC) approach is an Afrocentric approach or method of teaching science and technology developed in 2019 by a Nigerian scholar Professor Peter Akinsola Okebukola. The CTC approach postulates that for learning to take place, three elements such as the culture, the technology and the context of the teaching have to be greatly considered by the teacher. Okebukola's CTC approach is an amalgam, drawing on the power of three frameworks- (a) cultural context in which all learners are immersed; (b) technology-mediation to which teachers and learners are increasingly dependent; and (c) locational context which is a unique identity of every school and which plays a strong role in the examples and local case studies for lessons. Okebukola concludes that all the 20th-century tools for teaching science are not sufficiently appropriate for 21st-century teaching. Society is changing; the learner is changing; the teacher and teaching methods need to adjust to such changes. CTCA is, therefore a product of the desire to respond to the ever-changing school climate. On a concluding note, Okebukola expects CTCA to be an addition to the numerous tools available to the teacher. There is emerging evidence to its efficacy in promoting meaningful learning if properly used in the teaching-learning process.

Okebukola's Culturo-Techno-Contextual approach can be implicated to the paradigm shift in lecture delivery methods in 21st-century Cameroonian universities during the COVID-19 pandemic lockdown. Two major teaching methods were adopted by universities in Cameroon and supported by the government to sustain teaching-learning activities during the lockdown. These methods include; online teaching (e-learning- which is technology-based) and the blended teaching-learning methods. From Okebukola's cultural context, Cameroon universities operate in an internet era and majority of them are driven by a growing culture of Information Communication Technologies (ICTs) in which the average university student and staff are supposed to be adequately immersed. According to the World Bank (2017), the percentage of internet users in Cameroon rose from 5.74 in 1990 to 23.2 in 2017, with majority of the users being the youth of which a greater percentage should be university staff and students for obvious reasons. In terms of techno-mediation, the average student and university staff in the country has a computer laptop which they can averagely use in internet search and other online learning activities. The Ministry of Higher Education had from 2017 acquired 500,000 mini laptop computers and distributed to registered university students in the country.

Apart from possessing computer laptops, the average university staff and student in Cameroon are in possession of smart phones and are adequately grounded in operating and making use of them to access the internet and communicate through different social media and learning platforms. With these, it is therefore expected that a greater percentage of students and staff were ready and comfortable to embrace the paradigm shift from face-to-face classroom lecture delivery to online teaching and learning using the different e-learning platforms, especially the popular and commonly used ones.

Cameroon Universities in the Face of COVID-19 Pandemic Lockdown

Generally, universities are educational institutions of higher learning with an indispensable tri-function mandate (teaching, research and outreach/ community service) towards developing knowledge-based societies and economies for sustainable development. That is, they are engines of knowledge production, discovery, innovation, skills development, cultural preservation, and national progress (World Bank, 2020). The implication here is that there is an indispensable correlation between university education and sustainable economic and societal development (Ngwa and Fonkeng, 2017). According to the World Bank (2020), experiences of COVID-19 disruption to tertiary education exposed many significant short and long-term challenges facing tertiary education systems and institutions, including diminished resources for institutions, personal and academic challenges for institutions and students, demand for improved infrastructure to support continued distance and blended learning models, reduced mobility placing pressures to improve regional and local tertiary institutions, amongst others.

The COVID-19 pandemic lockdown in Cameroon as an emergency, created a paradigm shift in teaching/teaching methods within the country's universities. Though in an era of Information Communication Technologies (ICTs), the traditional form of teaching in Cameroon Universities, like in most Universities south of the Sahara prior to the COVID-19 lockdown has often involved face-to-face lectures given by academic staff to large groups of students. This is accompanied by large group tutorials, group laboratory sessions and workshops, with some independent study methods (Tambo, 2003). Even though the University of Buea has since 2008/2009 offered a first-degree program in Nursery and Primary Education through the Distance Education mode, it has however not involved any online teaching-learning methods and platforms. Thus, one cannot comfortably conclude that the University of Buea was already involved in some form of online teaching before the COVID-19 lockdown. What were the lecture delivery methods adopted by these institutions during the lockdown and how effective was the implementation? What problems were encountered in the application of these teaching methods and what prospects are there for improvements?

At the dawn of independence, the need for higher education to prepare the indigenous citizens for post-independence nation-building was a national priority, as was the case elsewhere in post-colonial Africa (Fonkeng, 2010). Consequently, the state of affairs in the country's higher education sector, particularly at the then lone Federal University of Cameroon located in Yaoundé in the early years of post-independence Cameroon brought about a series of problems that ushered in the reforms of the early 90s. Decree No. 92/74 of 13th April 1992, and complemented by decree No. 93/034 of 19th January 1993 created five full-fledged public universities to supplement the University of Yaoundé and also made some changes within the University system. Today, the government still being guided by the 1993 reforms has created more universities totalling eight public institutions. They include the Universities of Yaoundé I & II, Buea, Dschang, Ngaoundere, Douala, Maroua and Bamenda (the first six universities having been born out of the 1993 reforms and the last two established in 2008 and 2010 respectively). Added to these eight universities, are two virtual universities, one of which is for the CEMAC sub-region and a centre for telemedicine (SUP INFOS, 2010 and Doh, 2012).

Paradigm Shift in Lecture Delivery Methods & its Implementation

Teaching and learning in Cameroon Universities during the COVID-19 lockdown was sustained through the adoption of two major lecture delivery methods to replace the traditional face-to-face large groups lecture methods. The two methods are: the online teaching-learning and the blended teaching-learning methods. These methods were unanimously adopted in an emergency key stakeholders' meeting on the eve of the lockdown, and chaired by Cameroon's Minister of Higher Education, Jacques Fame Ndongo. The stakeholders gathering was aimed at reviewing the issues and challenges posed by the pandemic to higher education and mapping out emergency strategies that could help sustain continuous teaching and learning, while also respecting measures put in place by the state to contain the spread of the virus. This was to be achieved while maintaining the standards of quality assurance, professionalization of training, employability of graduates and distance learning (Ministry of Higher Education - MINESUP, 2020).

At the end of the stakeholders meeting, the following measures were prescribed to all heads of public, private and international higher institutes of learning in the country and sanctioned by the Ministry of Higher Education:

1. The mobilization of information and communication technologies to continue online teaching-learning and training activities, given the digital tools already available to students at the higher educational level.

2. In terms of work-linked training, activities continue in the receiving professional structures according to the procedures prescribed by the establishments concerned.

3. University research was limited to essential activities in compliance with government regulations on the regrouping of people in order to avoid a blank academic year.

4. The modification and reorganization of the 2020 calendar for university examinations and competitive entrance examinations, as well as the 2019/2020 academic year.

5. Sports, cultural and civic activities for 2020, notably the University Games, University Festival of Arts and Culture (UNIFAC), and the University Academic and Orientation Fair (UAOF) were postponed to 2021.

6. Suspension of all campus activities open to the public and avoidance of all campus gatherings with number of persons exceeding 50.

7. The intensification of awareness raising methods within university communities through the classical and digital media as well as through posters and direct communication.

It is on the basis of the above measures that individual university administrations adopted the online teaching-learning and blended learning methods as emergency measures to sustain teaching-learning activities in their various institutions. The adoption of these methods by the different universities was largely dependent on the culturo-techno-contextual disposition of their institutions in terms of students and staff preparedness, and the availability and adequacy of the prerequisite infrastructures.

Implementation of the Online Teaching-Learning Method

Within the context of higher education, online teaching-learning also known as E-learning or virtual classes refers to courses offered by higher institutions of learning completely through virtual platforms. According to Kentor (2015), online teaching-learning takes place over the internet, which is different from the traditional face-to-face lecture method in a brick-and-mortar university lecture hall. Majority of modern-day universities and students especially in the western world make use of Learning Management System (LMS) in their online pedagogic activities – which is a software application for maintaining, delivering, and tracking educational resources.

The use of LMS in this 21st century is coupled with other live digital learning platforms. These digital technologies and platforms that support present-day online pedagogy have continued to evolve with the evolution of distance education theories (Kentor, 2015). Some of these modern online learning technologies and platforms include; emails, telephone calls, google classroom, zoom, telephone conferencing, Social Media Chat Forums like Whatsapp, Facebook and video conferencing through Skype etc. Following the swift transition to online learning by many global universities as a result of the coronavirus pandemic, a good number of institutions were able to sustain teaching-learning activities through their LMS and some of these new digital learning technologies (Lau, Yang and Dasgupta, 2020). Scholars like Giesbers, Rienties, Tempelaar, and Gijselaers, (2014) argue that online learning environments offer a greater degree of flexibility than the traditional classroom settings. They have more diverse representations of student populations as learners prepare for working in the twenty-first century society. Such diversity comes from students' interaction with their surrounding geographical location, possibly offering a variety of perspectives on course content (Stewart, Harlow, and DeBacco, 2011).

Online lectures in Cameroon universities followed the same methods, those with already existing LMS decided to put them to use immediately, while those that did not have such platforms urgently developed them for the academic staff, students and the university administration to have a teaching-learning interaction and supervision of instructions. However, there was a great limitation in the implementation of this newly adopted innovation. Teachers and students had to be trained on how to make use of this innovation before they could register and begin engaging in effective teaching-learning interactions. Others, however, organized training on campus in shifts where academic staff were offered basic training on how to use the platform in teaching.

The University of Bamenda (UBa), in the North West Region of Cameroon for instance, introduced Moodle (UBa E-Learning) as its LMS, and organized faculty/school face-to-face small group trainings on Campus for academic staff. Nevertheless, the students had no formal or official training on how to make use of the UBa E-Learning platform stalling its effective utilization by staff and students during the lockdown.

In an opinion sample conducted amongst some eight (8) academic staff across different departments of the University of Bamenda, nearly all of them noted that the staff capacity building organized by the university administration on the use of the UBa Moodle platform was not enough to provide them with adequate skills on its effective use. Moreover, the inability of students to register and make use of the platform made it difficult for the staff to also make use of it as an online teaching-learning platform. One of the staffs stated that:

> *"...the training on how to use the UBa online learning platform did not include students and I don't know if they had a separate training. But what I can say is that I have not been able to use it to teach during this COVID-19 period. No student has signed any of my courses online and I cannot be issuing instructions and uploading learning resources without an audience... it's like trying to give a lecture in an empty classroom"*

It is therefore, evident that majority of academic staff across the different universities in Cameroon had to make use of the most convenient and familiar online learning platforms at their disposal. Apart from teachers of UBa who adopted alternative platforms after failing to engage students on the UBa E-learning platform; popular opinion amongst the teachers of other universities shows that they mostly made use of more convenient digital platforms such as E-mails, WhatsApp Chat forums, Google Classroom and Zoom in their online teaching-learning interaction with students. Online learning resources such as e-books, journal articles, audio and video resources, recorded lectures, quizzes etc. were made available to students through these platforms. Lectures were also delivered through these platforms using live question and answer sessions, and discussions forums. At the University of Buea in the South West Region of Cameroon, an academic staff commented that:

> *"...we mostly used WhatsApp chat forums and google classrooms for our online learning during lockdown...in fact most students were familiar with WhatsApp. They knew very little about the google classroom platform.... I faced serious challenges trying to introduce them to it.... Because of this we had to create different chat forums on WhatsApp according to the different courses I taught and it is through this platform that we successfully had our lectures until we were called back on campus in June.... Though it was challenging, it was also a very interesting experience.... But I must confess that our nation still has a long way to go so far as online learning is concern.... We're not yet there; we shouldn't only wait for coronavirus before we introduce digital innovations like online learning in our pedagogy."*

Implementation of the Blended Teaching-Learning Method

Blended learning is the combination of traditional classroom teaching with online learning and independent study which allows students to have more control over the time, pace and style of their learning. It is also considered as a combination of traditional face-to-face modes of instruction with online modes of learning, drawing on technology-mediated instruction, where all participants in the learning process are separated by a distance at some time (Siemens, Gašević, and Dawson, 2015). Empirical evidence has also concluded that students' achievement is higher in blended learning experiences when compared to either fully online or fully face-to-face experiences (Siemens, Gašević, and Dawson, 2015).

Looking at the above concept of blending learning, one can comfortably say that the most dominant alternative lecture delivery method by Cameroon Universities during the COVID-19 lockdown was blended learning. There was a mixture of online learning and amended face-to-face method in order to cover some of the limitations of the typical online learning system. This is especially as the change was swift and most staff were not prepared to embrace the change. After offering online lectures and exercises, teachers gave students independent learning tasks, group assignments and laboratory works. There was no way the students could effectively execute some of these tasks without a face-to-face encounter with some of the teachers for supervision. Considering the difficulty in incorporating laboratory work, and in some cases internships in online teaching, students were however assigned to laboratories and fieldworks in small groups with supervisors to follow up their learning activities in the laboratories and industrial sector. The students were however expected to work strictly under the COVID-19 prevention measures put in place by the state and executed by the different organizations and institutions. If the 2019/2020 academic year in Cameroon universities was rescued amidst the coronavirus disease, it is thanks to blended learning. The online teaching innovation could only accommodate teaching and continuous assessment, as summative assessments were done on campuses after the relaxation of lockdown rules by government authorities.

Problems Associated with the Implementation of Adopted Methods

The paradigm shift from face-to-face classroom lectures to the online lecture delivery method as a result of the coronavirus pandemic had far reaching challenges which by implication also affected the quality of teaching-learning activities. The fundamental challenges include amongst others: gross inadequate online learning infrastructure, non-preparedness of staff and students for online teaching and learning, resistance to change by some academic staff, inequality and non-inclusivity of online learning and difficulties in engaging in laboratory work and internship through online learning.

Gross inadequacy and non-availability of online learning infrastructure

Most countries had made investments in digital connectivity for decades which include fiberoptic infrastructure, provision of digital libraries, subsidized or free software, cloud services etc. Unfortunately, this is not the case with Cameroon. Added to the fact that there are nearly no independent university internet connections that could power connectivity on campuses and amongst stakeholders, staff and students had to ensure that online teaching and learning happened from their private resources. A good number of students had laptops, computers made available by the government but they couldn't use them to access online classes due to poor or complete absence of other online learning infrastructure on campuses and in the national territory as a whole. Some universities had never had an LMS and so only developed theirs when the need for online learning arose during the lockdown. Effective online learning therefore couldn't have been achieved under such an infrastructure lacking atmosphere.

Non- preparedness of staff and students for online learning

University academic staff and students in Cameroon lacked adequate training and skills on online learning skills. Most staff and students in Cameroon are very active on the online platform, but have never engaged in online teaching and learning before. Considering the fact that online learning had never been a serious policy issue in the country's universities prior to the COVID-19 pandemic, most staff and students did not have the necessary skills to fully embrace the innovation when it came. While some institutions employed a fire brigade approach to offer basic training to staff after the innovation, the training was not adequate to effectively equip the staff with the skills to do the job. Students were largely left out of such training and they had to study through discovery learning. This explains why many teachers and students jettisoned their individual university LMS platforms in favour of more convenient and conversant platforms for their online teaching-learning activities.

Resistance to change by academic staff

Renowned Canadian educational change expert Micheal Fulan noted that there will always be resistance to any change within the educational system from a section of stakeholders. Some members of the Cameroon academic class with a phobia for anything that requires the use of computer and other sophisticated technologies were not ready to accept online learning measures. They have become so comfortable with the traditional face-to-face lecture methods that they are prepared to retire with. It was therefore not an easy task getting this group of staff to get involved in the online teaching and learning. It is only thanks to blending that some of them had to cover their workloads for the semester.

Inequality and non- inclusivity of the methods

There was no equity and inclusivity in the online learning innovation when the international community is insisting on inclusion and sustainability especially in the education domain. Not all students and staff have access to connectivity and devices at home. This is particularly the case for the most remote and the poorest citizens who are university students. Digital divide therefore remains a serious issue between countries and within countries, amongst individuals. In Cameroon, poor internet coverage in rural and some urban areas makes online learning difficult. The innovation did not also take into consideration the needs of students with disabilities, especially those who require adapted computer services like students with visual impairment before having access to any online services.

Prospects for Improvements

The experience of Cameroon's tertiary institutions during the COVID-19 lockdown revealed that the nation has no emergency response plan and so not prepared for situations of emergency. There is therefore need for the development of a National Education Emergency Plan (NEEP) for Cameroon with short, medium- and long-term objectives or goals. The medium-term plan should prepare for post emergency reopening of educational institutions in situations of lockdown, building resilience and transformation, and making maximum use of available educational technologies where relevant and viable. The long-term plan should focus on building adequate and quality infrastructure and resources aimed at getting the educational system ready for pre-and post-emergency situations.

There is also need for strong capacity building for teachers on e-learning and the use of advance technologies that enhance teachers' capacity and capabilities for teaching and learning. Such training must not be offered only when there is need for teachers to demonstrate such skills, but the training must be part and parcel of frequently organized capacity building programs for staff by their various institutions.

Education leaders and stakeholders must collaborate to ensure that the teaching-learning process in universities produce high quality results. To achieve this, they must be prepared to embrace technological innovations, so that a change in lecture delivery methods from the traditional face-to-face to online platforms is able to deliver on the premise of learning and skills development. Leading the Tertiary Education sector towards post-crisis sustainability, will also require that education policy makers and practitioners focus more efforts on the most vulnerable students.

Conclusion

Governments across the world have relaxed the lockdown measures and economies are gradually opening back for business. But one thing is certain – history shall always note that between 2019 and 2020, the world was hit by an emergency- the COVID-19 pandemic in which all sectors of human life were grounded. The education sector, notably higher education and training which is critical for the revival and sustainability of nations including Cameroon was also grounded. The paradigm shift from the traditional face-to-face classroom lecture methods to the online and blended learning methods in Cameroon's higher education institutions was, therefore, an emergency response to sustain the higher education sector for post-pandemic and post-lockdown recovery as was the case elsewhere. The culturo-techno-contextual disposition of Cameroon's higher education institutions, including staff and students, appeared suited for the adoption of the online learning innovation. The multiple problems encountered in the online learning method and to a greater extent the success of blended learning implicationally revealed the huge gaps that still need to be filled for Cameroonian universities to have a sustainable e-learning system.

References

Cooperazione Internazionale (COOPI), (2019). *Education Emergency Policy.*

Dahlstrom, E; Brooks, D. C and Bichsel, J. (2014). *The current ecosystem of Learning Management Systems in Higher Education: Student, faculty, and IT perspectives.* Available at: https://library.educause.edu/resources/2014/9/the-current-ecosystem-of-learning-management-systems-in-higher-education-student-faculty-and-it-perspectives

Dede, C. (2007). *Transforming education for the 21st Century: New Pedagogies that Help All Students Attain Sophisticated Learning Outcomes.* Harvard University

Doh, S. P. (2012). *The Responses of the Higher Education Sector in the Poverty Reduction Strategies in Africa: The Case of Cameroon.* University of Tampere: Tampere University Press

Fonkeng, G. E and Ntembe, A. N. (2009). "Higher education and economic development in Africa: The case of Cameroon". *Educational Research and Review, 4, (5), 231-246.* Available online at: http://www.academic journals.org/ERR

Giesbers, B.; Rienties, B.; Tempelaar, D.; Gijselaers, W. (2014). "A dynamic analysis of the interplay between asynchronous and synchronous communication in online learning: The impact of motivation". *Journal of Computer Assisted Learning. 30 (1): 30–50. doi:10.1111/jcal.12020*

Graham, C. R.; Woodfield, W.; Harrison, J. B. (2013). "A framework for institutional adoption and implementation of blended learning in higher education". *The Internet and Higher Education. Blended Learning in Higher Education: Policy and Implementation Issues. 18: 4–14.* doi: 10.1016/j.iheduc.2012.09.003

INEE. (2009). *Pocket guide to inclusive education: Education in Emergencies: Including Everyone.* Avaialble at: http://www.ine.cl/

Jua, B. N. and Nyamjoh, F. B. (2002). "Scholarship Production in Cameroon: Interrogating a Recession". *African Studies Review, 45, (2), 49-71.*

Kentor, H. (2015). "Distance education and the evolution of online learning in the United States". *Curriculum and Teaching Dialogue.* 17: 21–34.

Lau, J., Yang, B and Dasgupta, R. (2020). *Will the coronavirus make online education go viral?* Available at: https://www.timeshighereducation.com/features/will-coronavirus-make-online-education-go-viral

Lawyer B. N. (2020). *Pedagogic Practices for Twenty First Century Teachers.* BeNti Print Buea\Kumba.

Longshurt, J. (2014). *Higher education for sustainable development. Guidance for UK education providers.* The Quality Assurance Agency for Higher Education: UK, London

MINESUP (2020). *Covid-19: Higher Education Stakeholders Preventive Measures.* Retrieved in August 2020 from: https://www.minesup.gov.cm/site/index.php/2020/03/31/circular-letter-of-march-21-2020-relating-to-preventive-and-control-measures-against-coronavirus-covid-19-in-the-higher-education-system/

Moskal, P.; Dziuban, C.; Hartman, J. (2012). "Blended learning: A dangerous idea?" *Internet and Higher Education. 18: 15–23. doi: 10.1016/j.iheduc.2012.12.001*

New Era (2020). Higher education 'must adapt to new normal.' *University World News: The Global Window on Higher Education.* Retrieved on August, 2020 from: https://www.universityworldnews.com/post.php?story=20200711141535122

Ngwa, E. S and Fonkeng, G. E. (2017). "Indigenous funding strategies for sustainable higher education in Cameroon". *African Journal of Social Sciences, 8 (3), 25 - 44.*

Ngwa, E. S. and Mekolle, P. M. (2020). "Public Policy on Education in Contemporary Cameroon: Perspectives, Issues and Future Directions". *European Journal of Education Studies, 7 (8), 187 - 205. DOI: 10.46827/ejesv7i8.3203.* Available at: www.oapub.org/edu

Ngwana, T. A. (2001). *The Implementation of the 1993 Higher Education Reforms in Cameroon: Issues and Promises.* Retrieved on 9th June, 2016 from: www.academia.edu

Ngwana, T. A. (2003). "University Strategic Planning in Cameroon: What Lessons for Sub- Saharan Africa?" *Education Policy Analysis Archives, 11(47).*

Njeuma, D. L. (2003). "Cameroon". In D. Teferra & P. G. Altbach (eds.), Higher Education: An International Reference. Indiana University Press, 215–223. Available at: http://www.bc.edu/bc_org/avp/soe/cihe/ inhea/ profiles/ Cameroon.htm

Nwaimah, T. E. (2008). "CAMEROON: New university part of tertiary reforms". *University World News, Issue No. 15.* Retrieved from: www.university worldnews.com

Oben, J., Bigoga, J., Takuissu, G. and Leke, R. (2020). *The Potential Use of a Cameroonian Functional Food (Star Yellow) to Curb the Spread of the COVID-19 Via Feces.* Cambridge Open Engage

Okebukola, A. P. (2019). *The Culturo-Techno-Contextual (CTC) Approach.* Retrieved on August, 2020 from: http://ctcapproach.com/#

Siemens, G., Gašević, D., & Dawson, S. (2015). *Preparing for the Digital University: a review of the history and current state of distance, blended, and online learning.* Athabasca University. Retrieved from: http://linkresearchlab.org/PreparingDigitalUniversity.pdf

Stewart, A. R., Harlow, D. B., and DeBacco, K. (2011). "Students' experiences of synchronous learning in distributed environments". *Distance Education. 32 (3): 357–381.*

Sunjo, E. T., Wuyt, A. K., and Saidu, Y. (2020). *Lockdown Preventive Measure Against COVID-19 Pandemic: Livelihoods Implications in Cameroon.* Nkafu Policy Institute

SUP INFOS (2010). A Bilingual Quarter Review of Higher Education in Cameroon. No. 14, MINESUP Yaoundé, Cameroon.

Tambo, L. I. (2003). *Principles & Methods of Teaching: Applications in Cameroon Schools.* Buea: ANUCAM Publishers

Tambo, L. I. (2003b). *Cameroon National Education Policy Since the 1995 Forum.* Limbe: Design House

UN (2010). *United Nations General Assembly Resolution on the Right to Education in Emergency Situations (2010).* UNO.

UNESCO (2019). *Education in Emergencies.* Available at: https://en.unesco.org/themes/education-emergencies

UNHCR (2019). *Education in Emergencies.* Available at: https://emergency.unhcr.org/entry/53602/education-in-emergencies

World Health Organization (W.H.O) (2020). *Coronavirus disease (COVID-19) pandemic.* Available at: https://www.who.int/emergencies/diseases/novel-coronavirus-2019

World Bank (2017). *Cameroon: Internet Users 1990-2017.* Retrieved in August 2020 from: https://www.theglobaleconomy.com/Cameroon/Internet_users/

World Bank (2020). *The COVID-19 Crisis Response: Supporting tertiary education for continuity, adaptation, and innovation.* World Bank Group. Retrieved in August 2020 from: http://pubdocs.worldbank.org/en/621991586463915490/WB-Tertiary-Ed-and-Covid-19-Crisis-for-public-use-April-9.pdf

6

Pearls and Pitfalls of Online Teaching during Covid-19 Pandemic: Indian Perspective

Jayanta Das

Abstract

The chapter examines the pearls and pitfalls of online teaching and learning during covid-19 pandemic in India. 11th March 2020 changed the whole world. The World Health Organization (WHO) announced COVID-19 outbreak as a pandemic. Suddenly human civilization landed at an uncertain crossroad. The death toll due to the pandemic affected the whole world. Social distancing became the new social norm. Geopolitical turmoil and its socioeconomic impact didn't leave any sector untouched with the educational institutions hardest hit. The chapter argues that digital education appears to be a viable solution to fill in the void for classroom education during COVID-19 period while minimizing the chances of getting infected. The study reveals that online education is still in the nascent stage in India and no one was prepared. However, in the future, digital education is likely to be incorporated into mainstream education. This will enable inclusive education by facilitating learning across diverse geographies in India. Moreover, it will provide an opportunity for educators to come up with customized learning solutions for every student. Though in this pandemic situation, India adopted online teaching by default, not by choice, it has an immense beneficial role for all the stakeholders, including students and teachers.

Introduction - Understanding Education

Many great philosophers attempted to define 'education' and amongst them, I would like to mention Swami Vivekananda. He said: "Education is the manifestation of all perfection already in man." If we emphasize the definition given by Swami Vivekananda, we will find the three main concepts, firstly 'the manifestation', secondly, 'perfection' and thirdly, 'already in man.' As time evolved since the beginning of human civilization, people became better educated to realize the meaning of education as Swami Vivekananda envisioned in the following manner:

Manifestation: Expression or application of the knowledge and skill for survivability and sustainability. This was also echoed by many scientists including Charles Darwin (survivability of the fittest). All the knowledge and skills acquired and utilized through neuropsychological and physical manner at personal level and integration with others at social level depending on NLP (neuro linguistic programming).

Perfection: The state of being perfect or faultless in a specified time frame, in a principle of mutatis mutandis. Therefore 'perfect' is never a fixed point or line rather than 'infinitesimally faultless.'

Already in man: The knowledge and skill human acquired (learned) till that point of time, for better survivability in the universe. Evolutionary processes and genetic transmission is the evidence in front of us.

Foundation of education based on rational implementation of ND-PMS-3B (Where 'ND' means Need and Desire; 'PMS' means physical, mental and social; '3B' means being, belonging and becoming).

Therefore, education is the progressive cyclical journey towards eternity for survivability, sustainability and supremacy.

Unitary, Identity and Integration

All education starts with our identification in the given perspective, starting from one individual to gradually bigger circles of the universe. Here, *'Identity'* is defined as, certain unique characteristics by which we can separate the thing from the rest of the world or universe, by exclusion of the thing under consideration. We may start from either direction though it's easier to start from oneself and gradual integration with his surrounding of bigger circles. That integration manifests as rationality of being as part of the surrounding. Philosophically all the human civilizations followed the same path. As we approach towards bigger circle we face newer challenges and phenomenon which we tried to understand with our existing knowledge. If we fail to understand with existing knowledge, begin a search for explanation and till we are not satisfied. This gives birth of new knowledge aligned with 'necessity is the mother of invention'. To propagate the knowledge to the next generation we also developed methods for making others understand. Thus, explaining that nature gave birth of 'science' and communicating to others gave birth of 'arts' are the two primary subjects of human civilization. The eternal question 'why' actually gave us the answer of fundamental questions of the universe. The famous story of Sir Isaac Newton and the drop of the apple gave us the answer of what we know as gravitation. All scientific explanations start from the same fundamental question, why? After having a satisfactory explanation, humans try always to copy or manipulate that for the sake of our benefit. Using scientific understanding for the better living of mankind gave birth of technology. Whatever is the technology it stems from manipulating the nature for human benefit. Commerce developed later, and actually designed for self-benefits utilizing science, technology and arts. The world we live in today is driven by commerce and all the functional units integrated with that. Principally science and technology gave the human advantage over other types of living and the nonliving world; whereas commerce divided human into various 'sub-units'; in various names like country / race / class / community etc.

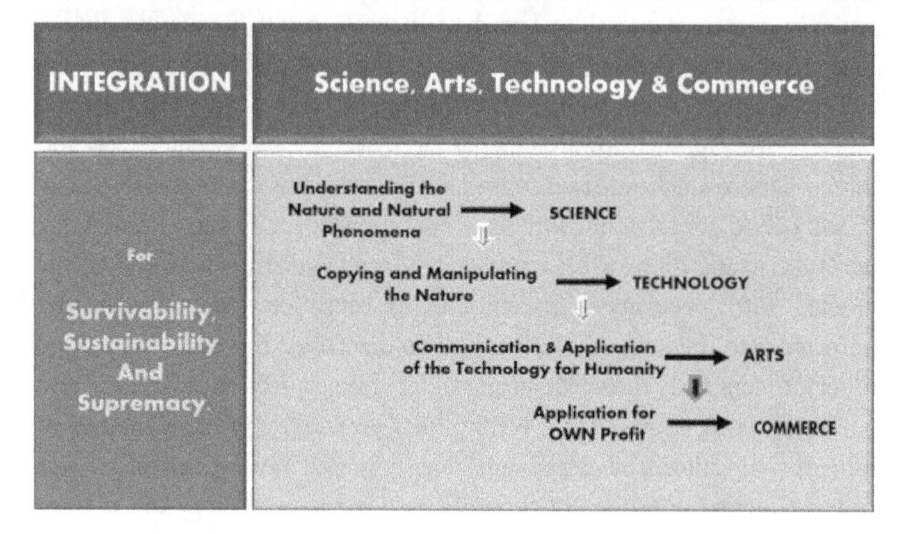

Figure 5. Correlation of fundamental subjects. Source: Jayanta Das, October 2020.

All the subjects we know today are developed to give tangibility of previously intangible things. Here the tangibility refers beyond its literary meaning 'touchable.' Rather, it means expression of quality with quantification. If I say Bob is a tall guy then the interpretation will vary from region to region; but if I mention Bob is 6 feet tall then throughout the world all will interpret the same height. Thus 'numbers' as unit and 'mathematics' as subject give the highest tangibility and considered as mother of all subjects. Thus, to give better tangibility, 'unit' is the key.

Principles of Education

Education is a deliberate conscious process for undertaking organized and coordinated rational human behaviours. In that way, its goal oriented and designed to attain. Philosophy of education that poses questions on the human activity and engagement, germinated from the principles of education. Principles are the essence of existence of the entity, which can't be separated. The principle is a general or universal rule that applies to several specific manifestations of such an entity, that must always be present for that thing to go on existing, or else that thing will stop existing. An entity is any being, including a person, an object, an event or a situation. For instance, hunger and starvation in any country is a situational entity which means the shortage of food. The principle is an abstract constant that underlies or forms the foundation of specific objects, events or situations. In the given example, 'shortage of food' is the principle underlying the situational entity hunger and starvation. Principle has three major dimensions, which means:

i) It's the reason of existence of the entity

ii) It's the meaning to the entity they underlie

iii) It's the rule that enables the entity to integrate with other entities.

Thus if we corroborate this with education we will be able to understand the five major components as principles of education;

i) Metaphysics – concerned with questions on reality

ii) Epistemology - concerned with questions on knowledge

iii) Axiology - concerned with questions on value

iv) Logic - concerned with sound reasoning

v) Manifestation – concerned with rational behavioral aspects.

Teaching as Delivery of Education

Teaching is one of the oldest Nobel professions and the teachers took the pain to groom the human to the civilized society we belong today. It is the highest multidimensional activity requiring social, economic, scientific and technological dimensions. Teaching is the vehicle of transferring existing knowledge and skills to the next generation along with the quest for the newer knowledge and skills. As education has no defined boundary, the horizon of teaching also has no boundary. Rather, it is an effort to integrate 'micro to macro similarity'.

According to the empiricism theory (epistemological), the only source of genuine knowledge is through our sensory experiences. This means what we see, hear, touch, smell or taste. The mind is like a blank hard drive upon which experience makes its marks. Without sensory experiences we would not know specific features in the world around us. We have ability to conceive qualities such as colours, odours, sounds or musical notes and tastes only through sensory inputs. Without taste buds we cannot tell whether the food we are eating has too much salt or not. If one has no taste buds one cannot conceive how bitter quinine is, or how sweet honey is. Empiricism contends that reason is grounded on the solid rock of sensory experiences.

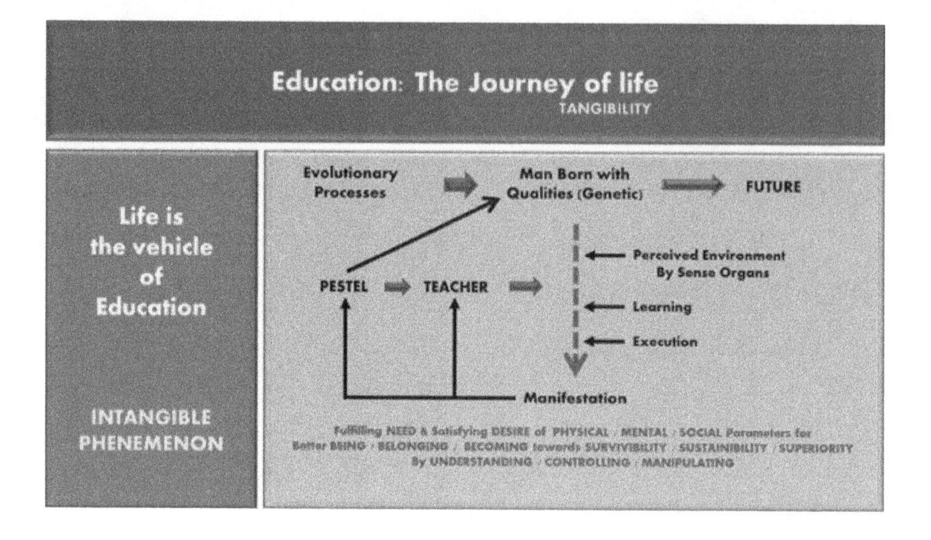

Figure 6. The process of teaching and learning. Source: Jayanta Das, October 2020.

From the pre-historic time, teaching was based on verbal communication and memorization of the other end. With the progress of our society, humans and their environment have also developed up to the standard of what we are experiencing today. Nowadays, formal education is an organized system and technologically enhanced for better outcome in a progressive cyclical way. The main function of teaching is not only to teach but it is also to measure outcome and analyze for further betterment of all the taxonomical entities. This is done as follows:

a) Cognitive domain

i) Retention or memorization of knowledge

ii) Comprehension or understanding

iii) Application

iv) Analysis

v) Synthesis and

vi) Evaluation.

b) Affirmative domain

i) Receiving

ii) Responding

iii) Valuing

iv) Organization

v) Characterization by value or value set

c) Psychomotor domain

i) Reflex Movements

ii) Basic Fundamental Movements

iii) Perceptual Abilities

iv) Physical Abilities

v) Skilled Movements

vi) Non-discursive or Coherent Communication

Therefore, in a structured environment, teaching is not only limited to the delivery of education but also includes assessment for outcome in a sustainable way for a better future.

Our Academic System

The fundamental questions of education 5WH (why, what, who, when, whom and how) gave birth of various newer subjects starting from science and arts. As education and teaching progressed over the period of time, the structured assessment-based teaching took place through the academic institutions. That is our academic system through which we are groomed, starting from schools to universities. Institutions have physical existence and both the teachers and students have all the ND-PMS-3B parameters in line. Gradually, national and other policies took control over the whole system of education and teaching. Whether that is good or bad, is beyond the scope of this chapter. Grossly, the modern structured education and teaching is designed to produce required workforce for the society and mostly Government regulated. Moreover, research activities are Government or corporate regulated for respective unitary benefits.

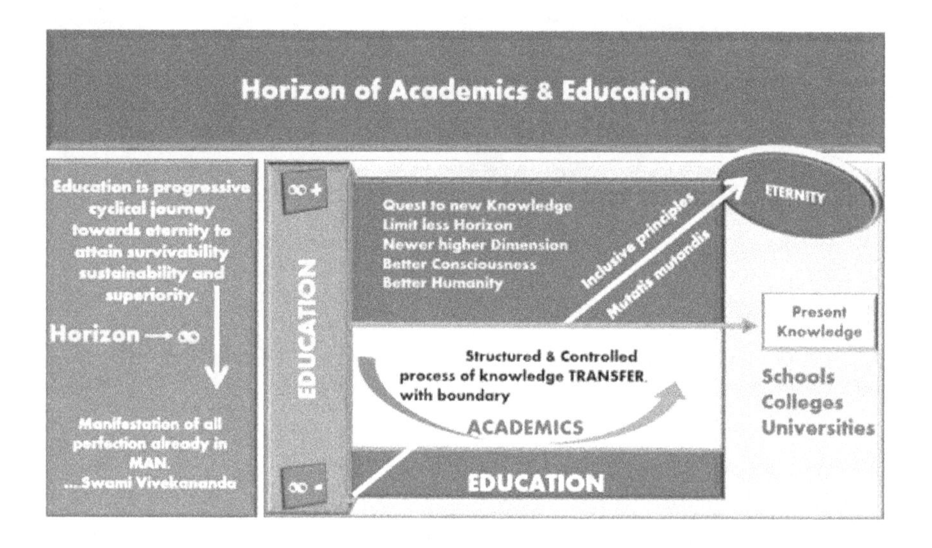

Figure 7. Horizons of education. Source: Jayanta Das, October 2020.

COVID- 19 and Paradigm Shift in Education and Teaching in India

As lockdown and social distancing enforced by Governments due to the corona virus pandemic, the academic institutions were and are kept closed by most of the countries. India is not an exception. This situation led to many teaching challenges on students and teachers as well as the overall society. According to the Human Rights Watch report, more than 1.5 billion students are already out of school. Widespread job and income loss along with economic insecurity among families are likely to also increase child labor, sexual exploitation, and teen pregnancies among other woes. Most of the Governments and corporate houses adopted policy of work from home (WFH). In India, there are about 91% of students presently out of school, ranging from nursery to university. For the time being, the academic institutions switched to online teaching as the only option left in the pandemic. Even the Government came up with eLearning solutions. Amongst them, worth of mentioning are Diksha, e-*Pathshala*, (e-school) NROER (National Repository of Open Educational Resources), *Swyam*,(Own) e-PG *Pathshala*. Many big Tech institutions and companies also jumped to find out the way-out. Nevertheless, COVID-19 pandemic forced experts to rethink the conventional methods of education. Digital education appears to be a viable solution to fill in the void for classroom education for the pandemic period while minimizing the chances of getting infected. More importantly, online education is still in nascent stage in India and no one was prepared. In the future, digital education is likely to be incorporated into mainstream education. This will enable inclusive education by facilitating learning across diverse geographies in India. Moreover, it will provide an opportunity for educators to come up with customized learning solutions for every student.

Though in this pandemic situation, India adopted online teaching by default, not by choice; still it has immense beneficial role for all the stakeholders, including students and teachers. The positive impacts of online teaching are as follows:

i) **A move towards online learning:** COVID-19 has acted as positive catalyst for adoption of digital technologies to deliver education. Academic Institutions moved towards blended mode of learning. It encouraged both the teachers and students to become more tech savvy. New ways of teaching and assessments of learning opened new opportunities for a major transformation in the area of curriculum development and pedagogy. It also gives access to large number of learners at a time.

ii) **Increased use of learning management system:** Use of LMS (learning management systems) by educational institutions became high demand. It opened a great opportunity for the companies that have been developing and upgrading learning management systems for the use of educational institutions. Even many startups also rising in a very prominent way.

iii) **Increased use of soft copy of study materials:** The academic institutions are closed for safety. The students are not able to collect the hard copies of study materials and hence most of the students used soft copy materials for reference. Indirectly, it reduced paper wastage in a significant way.

iv) **Rise in online meetings and seminars:** Webinar took place of the physical meetings. It did not only help to prevent the spread of COVID-19 but is also economical.

v) **Enhances in digital collaboration and data transfer:** Email made letter writing almost a lost art. Various technological methods of online data transfer enables faster and convenient data transfer in few seconds which was unthinkable.

vi) **Increased digital literacy and competency:** Necessity increased both the digital literacy and competency in a short period of time.

vii) **Global exposure in fingertips:** Digital access made the whole world just like a village. We may have information in just few clicks.

viii) **Overcoming geographical barrier and better time management:** India is a vast country with many geographical extremes. Online teaching easily can overcome the geographical barrier ably connect a large number of students at a time.

ix) **Increased demand for Open and Distance Learning (ODL):** Most of the students prefer the ODL as it enhances self-learning at convenience. Many authentic sources also provide free of cost. NPTEL online courses are one of such greatest examples.

Challenges Faced in Online Teaching

Online teaching in India had short term severe disruption of face-to-face teaching. It turned up into a massive shock wave in teachers' productivity as well as students' learning and social life which may leave long term consequences. The major challenges faced in India are as follows:

1. **We were not ready:** In India, we were depending on traditional classroom-based education system. In our institutions, none (teachers and students) were prepared to abruptly switch to online. Though few institutions were well equipped, that was not even peanuts compared to the quantum requirements needed. Before this pandemic, the efforts and investments towards infrastructural development of online education was practically invisible both from Government and corporate side. Though few institutions

might have the facilities with some degree of teacher's and student's digital awareness, that is largely not the scenario throughout India.

2. **Technological issues:** Online teaching requires high-end technology and gazettes like computers, internet etc. which are not available across all the socioeconomic strata. Moreover, user interphase requires special knowledge and skill. We have not trained our teachers as well as, students with online education. Besides, electricity supply is not uniformly distributed throughout the country. India needs structured teachers' training programs though they are costly and time consuming.

3. **Economic issues:** Many students simply can't afford the technology required for online education. Inequality among students became evident. Moreover, economic slowdown impacted on all the stakeholders. Several parents are facing difficulties in COVID-19 pandemic due to job loss or pay cut. It is becoming difficult to maintain families due to uneven distribution of wealth across the societies. Both the availability and affordability are in question. The sudden rise in the price of essential goods and services made the situation worse. Apart from few online service providers, and those supplying essential goods and services, none made good business. The social stigma of COVID-19 affected families and uncertainty also played a role indirectly. Many academic institutions faced financial crunch due to nonpayment of fees and authorities tried to manage by pay cuts from teachers. This remedy actually proved counterproductive in the overall education system. Many specialized education sectors such as hotel management, travel and tourism etc. are purely job oriented. They are having extreme negative impact.

4. **Physical activity and health issues:** As none of the teachers or students are coming to the institutions, no physical activity is there which is an essential part of the growth and development of the students. Moreover, continuous sitting in front of computer screens gives rise to eye problems, headache, neck pain, backache, sleep disturbances, obesity, etc.

5. **Social activity issues:** Online education is done in isolation. Lack of social interactions causes stress, depression and fatigue. In India

the 'mid-day meal' attracted many students from marginalized and economically challenged section of society. Stress, anxiety, uncertainty and lack of Government initiatives caused more social unrest. Though some unofficial reports suggest that schools may open by the October, 2020, it implies that a good part of the year will be lost. There is no news on financial support to schools, while petitions backed by politicians against schools' interests keep growing. Many exams are still to happen. Outgoing batches find difficulty to get a job as there is much less opportunity at this moment. In the near future the job market would drastically change and new types of knowledge and skill will be required to sustain.

6. **Effective learning issues:** It's the most important challenge in online education. The effective teaching and learning depend on cognitive, affirmative and psychomotor domains. Though online teaching is trying to get best possible output, it is really difficult without face-to-face interactions.

   a) None of the barriers of learning (the *critical-logical* barrier, the *intuitive-emotional* barrier and the *critical-moral* barrier) could be addressed properly.

   b) Isolation makes students passive learners and no control over distractions. Too much flexibility makes them less focused. Engagement and collaboration are difficult.

   c) Preparation of study material is time consuming and costly affair.

   d) Uncertainty of future giving rise of anxiety.

   e) Assessment is difficult as there is no direct communication (as in class room).

7. **Skill based subjects can't be taught**: The subjects require practical hands-on training. For instance, Nursing, Engineering and Medicine etc. can't be taught online.

Adapting Changes in Teaching for Sustainability

Teachers are COVID-19 warriors. They engaged to reshape the future of the students for their better survivability, sustainability and supremacy, like a *Phoenix*. The principle of implementation is same UCM (understand, control and manipulate) model followed in everything, teaching is not an exception.

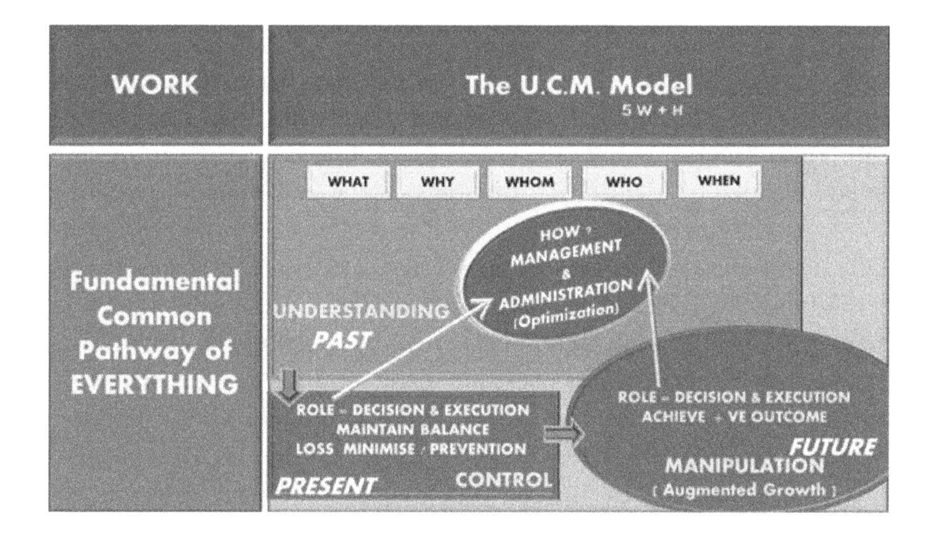

Figure 8. The UCM model. Source: Jayanta Das, October 2020.

The following measures are already incorporated in online teaching for better outcomes. They are:

1. Making the digital sessions dynamic by coordinating virtual group activities, allowing onscreen activity and voice, time bound attendance etc.

2. Keeping the learner busy by scheduled tasks with quantifiable outcome and accountability.

3. Making digital study material.

Clinical Medicine in COVID-19 Pandemic

Clinical medicine is the all-encompassing domain of health of an individual and society at large. Health is defined as, "state of complete *physical*, *mental* and social *wellbeing* and not just merely absence of any disease." In general, we do understand the '*physical*' component and healthcare focusses on that, though '*mental*' and '*social*' parameters are the larger pie. Even if, for the time being, we consider the '*physical*' parameter only, the pandemic made huge impact in healthcare system. In India, we do spend around 4% of GDP for healthcare whereas, advanced countries spend about 7 to 10% of their GDP. So, obviously resources are limited. During this pandemic a large number of citizens are sick at a time when there is limited infrastructure including health care personnel like doctors, nurse and supporting staff. On top of that, costly private healthcare and corruption at various levels made the situation worse. The credibility of various apex authorities (World Health Organisation, Centre for Disease Control, Indian Council of Medical Research etc.) are at stake due to confusing recommendations and guidelines. Social stigma and confusion regarding COVID-19 immensely impacted healthcare. Till the time of this article, i.e. October 2020, about 215 doctors died in India due to COVID-19. In many parts of India, doctors and other healthcare workers are not even getting their remunerations. There are many instances where neighbours are objecting the stay of doctors and other health care workers at their home or in the rented apartments. Many medical colleges are converted to COVID-19 hospitals. This jeopardized the usual academics and training of budding doctors. With all these adversities doctors, nurses and other healthcare workers are trying hard to get over the situation.

Conclusion

We are in the process of creative strategies to ensure that all students must have sustainable access to learning during pandemic COVID-19. Policies are being made by the various think tanks and individuals from diverse backgrounds for effective teaching. Standardized teaching and study material is the utmost importance for proper implementation. Gradual transformation from traditional to online teaching or a rational blend of the two is the key to overcome the impact of the pandemic. Immediate measures are required to handle the economic impact on the large section of the society. Every crisis brings some opportunities and thus there is a need to make proper use of it. As online practice is benefitting the students immensely, it should be continued. Further detailed statistical study may be undertaken to explore the long term impact of COVID-19 on the education system of India. Ideally speaking online teaching can be supplementary teaching method along with class room teaching. It is however significant to note that in spite of the many limitations of online teaching, it remains the only sustainable option for the time being and might be in the foreseeable near future.

References

A Jornet, WR Roth. (2016). Understanding Educational Psychology. Springer.

Bhujang Bobade, O Ligade. (1996). History of Indian Education.Atlantic Publishers.

Cooperman Larry. (2017). Art of Teaching Online: How to Start and How to succeed as an online Instructor. Chandos Publishers.

Darlene Christopher. (2014). Successful virtual Classroom: How to design and Facilitate Interactive and Engaging Live Online Teaching. Amacom Publishers.

Harasim. (2017). Learning Theory, Online technology. New York. Routledge Publishers.

Isabel, L.Beck, Linda Kucan,(2002).Bringing Words to life . Guilford Publisher.

Issac Asimov. (1983). The Roving Mind. Prometheus publishers.

John Hattie. (2008). Visible Learning: A Synthesis of over 800 Meta Analyses Relating to Achievement. Routledge Publishers.

Launcelot Brown, Gary Shank, J Pringle. (2018) Understanding Educational Research: A Guide to Critical reading. Rutledge Publishers.

N Jaypalan. (2007). Problems of Indian Education. Atlantic Publishers.

P Smeyers,R Smith .(2014).Understanding Education and Educational Research. UK.Cambridge university press.

Rita Marie, Judith V, Boettcher. (2010). The Online Teaching Survival guide: Simple Practical Pedagogical Tips. Routledge Publishers.

Swapnil Parikh,Maherra Desai,Rajesh Parikh .(2020).The Coronavirus :What You Need to Know About The Global Pandemic .Penguin e Bury Publishers.

Tiffany Jones. (2013) Understanding educational Policy: "Four Education Orientations Framework". New York. Springer.

WEB LINKS

https://en.wikipedia.org/wiki/Education ,on 30.9.20 ,7:39 pm

https://www.springer.com/gp/book/9789811064326, on 30.9.20,7:39 pm

https://infed.org/mobi/what-is-education-a-definition-and-discussion/, on 30.9.20,7:39 pm

https://scholar.harvard.edu/files/roychan/files/chan_r._y._2016._pdf on 30.9.20, 7:39 pm

https://unesdoc.unesco.org/images/0023/002348/234807e.pdfon 30.9.20, 7:39 pm

https://www.mhrd.gov.in/sites/upload_files/mhrd/files/NEP_Final_English_0.pdf on 30.9.20, 7:39 pm

https://www.unicef.org/publications/files/A_Human_Rights_Based_Approach_to_Education_for_All.pdf on 30.9.20, 7:39 pm

https://www.gcc.mass.edu/about/principles-of-education/ on 30.9.20,7:39 pm

https://gregashman.wordpress.com/2017/05/05/5-principles-of-education/ on 30.9.20, 7:39 pm

https://www.jstor.org/stable/7005 on 30.9.20, 7:39 pm

http://shodhganga.inflibnet.ac.in/bitstream/10603/112304/8/08_chapter%204.pdf on 30.9.20,7:39 pm

https://www.britishcouncil.in/sites/default/files/school_education_system_in_india_report_2019_final_web.pdf on 30.9.20 7:39 pm

http://www.evaldesign.com/uploads/2/3/8/2/23823775/school_education_india__evaldesign.pdf on 30.9.20, 7:39 pm

https://www.researchgate.net/publication/341844264_Confronting_Covid-19_with_a_Paradigm_Shift_in_Teaching_and_Learning_A_Study_on_Online_Classes on 1.10.20 3:00 pm

https://www.mdpi.com/2071-1050/12/14/5646/pdf on 1.10.20, 3:00 pm

https://gocoderz.com/blog/challenges-teachers-face-when-teaching-online/ on 1.10.20, 3:00 pm

https://jellyfish.tech/10-challenges-of-e-learning-during-covid-19/ on 1.10.20, 3:00 pm https://www.embibe.com/exams/online-learning-challenges-and-solutions/ on 1.10.20,3:00 pm

https://go.marybaldwin.edu/education/2018/02/23/teaching-online-challenges-solutions/ on 1.10.20 3:00 pm

https://www.researchgate.net/publication/319013030_Issues_and_Challenges_for_Teaching_Successful_Online_Courses_in_Higher_Education_A_Literature_Review on 1.10.20 , 3:00 pm

https://www.researchgate.net/publication/312182813_The_Challenges_of_Online_Learning_Supporting_and_Engaging_the_Isolated_Learneron 1.10.20,3:00pm

https://scalar.usc.edu/works/c2c-digital-magazine-spring--summer-2018/common-challenges-teaching-online on 1.10.20,3:00 pm

https://www.researchgate.net/publication/250167140_Characteristics_of_Sustainable_Changes_for_Schools on 1.10.20 ,3:00 pm

https://www.nejm.org/coronavirus on 1.10.20 , 3;00 pm

https://jamanetwork.com/journals/jamainternalmedicine/fullarticle/2768879 on 1.10 .20.3:00pm

https://blogs.biomedcentral.com/on-medicine/2020/05/15/the-clinical-trials-fighting-the-covid-19-pandemic/ on 3.10.20 ,12:04 pm

https://www.nature.com/articles/s41581-020-00336-9 on 3.10.20,12:04pm

https://www.jocmr.org/index.php/JOCMR/article/view/4142 on 3.10 ..20,12:04 pm

https://www.ncbi.nlm.nih.gov/pmc/articles/PMC7151405/ on 3.10.20, 12:04 pm

https://www.scielo.br/scielo.php? On 3.10.20, 12:04 pm

https://www.acponline.org/clinical-information/clinical-resources-products/coronavirus-disease-2019-covid-19-information-for-internists on 3.10.20,12:04 pm

https://www.researchgate.net/publication/340528239_Micro-Impact_of_the_Pandemic_by_Covid19_in_the_General_Medicine_Clinical_and_Epidemiological_Reflections_from_the_Situation_in_Spain_March_2020 on 3.10.20,12:04 pm

https://www.researchgate.net/publication/341074814_COVID-19_Considerations_for_Medical_Education_during_a_Pandemic on 3.10.,20, 12:04pm

https://jamanetwork.com/journals/jama/fullarticle/2764727 on 3.10.20,12:04 pm

https://www.who.int/publications-detail-redirect/clinical-management-of-covid-19 on 3.10.20,12:04pm

https://www.nejm.org/coronavirus on 3.10.20,12:04 pm

Section III

E-learning and Community Concerns During Pandemic

7

COVID-19 Lockdown and Online Classes: Challenges in ASEAN Countries

Sandeep Poddar

Abstract

Worldwide, an unprecedented 363 million children and youth are affected by closures of schools and universities, according to data released in March 2020 by the United Nations' education agency UNESCO. That number is expected to rise as more countries implement lockdowns. In Southeast Asia, several schools have been closed amid the worsening case of COVID 19 in the region, and many universities shifted in-person classes to online learning as an effort to limit further transmission of the pathogen. The study argues that the sudden change to online teaching has raised concerns among many teachers and professors in Southeast Asia. Even though the world has become hyper-connected and internet penetration continues to increase every year, a large segment of the population in Southeast Asia doesn't have access to the internet and electronic devices because many students are from economically vulnerable families. Their accesses to computers are limited to school-provided computer labs, and many do not have access to unlimited internet on their mobile devices. Internet penetration in Association of South East Asian Nations (ASEAN) is limited. The study reveals that only three countries have over 80 per cent Internet penetration, Singapore leading the statistics, followed by Brunei and then Malaysia. For countries like Indonesia, the most populous nation in the region, only 56 per cent (150 million) of its 268 million population have access to the internet. Thailand, Myanmar, and Vietnam have less than 60 per cent internet penetration, with 57 per cent, 39 per cent and 38 per cent respectively in 2019. Some International Schools, Colleges and Universities run online classes via different available platforms like Zoom, Team viewer, and give assignments. But as majority of students in rural area get very slow or no internet, the long-term sustainability of online education in all level is not feasible. Moreover, the Education sector is broadly divided in 4 segments, Preschool, Primary, Secondary and after school—College/ University Higher Education. Preschool prepares the habits; the primary school education is involved mainly with discipline, culture, social activity etc. scarcely delivered online. Secondary and Higher education focuses more on practical skill-based training such as vocational courses, Laboratory based and clinical or laboratory research based where online education could not be implemented 100%. For instance, in Health Sciences, Engineering etc. Usually, all higher education needs field based training and project. The use of internet affects mental health as well. So, in a nutshell the feasibility challenges or hurdles are more to complement the traditional teaching methods.

Introduction

Curricula and pedagogical practices reformation in the teaching of science, mathematics and technology by the integration of social dimension gained importance and broadened in scope and magnitude (Olson et al., 1999). The pedagogical innovations have been explored using information and communication technology at the school level (Harris, 2002; Janicki and Liegle, 2001; Martinez-Garcia et al., 2012; Hargis, 2001; Mioduser et al., 2003; Wu et al., 2008; & Law, 2006). Even if there are differences among countries in Asia and the Pacific, there are common experiences with regard to changes in approaches to education. Mainly the focus of attention in this study is the shifting from uniformity to diversity, from teacher-centered to learner-centered ones, and from examination-oriented learning to whole person development (Law & Miura, 2015).

In our education learning process, two major theories are common with its various attributes. They are the cognitive and non-cognitive theories. The cognitive theory is concerned with knowing and thinking. It studies the structures and components for processing information. The fields of study encompassed are memory, attention, perception, language, reasoning, problem solving and creativity (Elliott et al., 2000). The cognitive foundation of learning theory was initially based on the study of human 'memory', and it takes 'mental representation' as a central proposition. On the other hand, the non-cognitive attributes are skills and traits that are not specifically intellectual or analytical in nature. These skills are not directly related to specific subjects and contents. They include a range of personality and motivational habits and attitudes that facilitate functioning well in school and life, such as life skills, critical thinking, peaceful living, value-based living, perseverance, motivation, self-control, and other aspects of conscientiousness (Rosen, Glennie, Dalton, Lennon, & Bozick, 2010). The eight non-cognitive skills that are considered by Gutman (2013, p.7) as key competencies in the twenty-first century are as follows:

1. Self-perception
2. Motivation
3. Perseverance
4. Self-control
5. Meta-cognitive strategies
6. Social competencies
7. Resilience and coping
8. Creativity

With the increased use of ICTs around the globe, education systems are adapting new technology into the curriculum, to help to meet current demands in the education segment (Lo Bianco 2010). Aguilar (2012) mentioned that the alignment of technology with education practices is a positive step that has been triggered by issues such as transportation distances and building costs. In developing countries such as in ASEAN Regions, much research has been conducted. This is becoming one of the challenges since the number of students and teachers in developing countries are bigger than in developed countries. Moreover, the adoption of technology in developing countries is much greater due to the development of the latest software, hardware, and capabilities on electronic communications (Gaol & Hutagalung, 2020).

Globally, over 1 billion new internet users have been added over the last four years. However, substantial digital divides persist between more and less connected countries, communities, and people. In 2019, about 87 % of the people in developed countries were using the internet compared with 47% in developing countries. (ITU. 2019). During COVID-19 pandemic, out of the 1,058,824,335 affected learners, that is, 60.5% of the total enrolled learners, 106 country-wide closures have been identified (UNSECO, 2020).

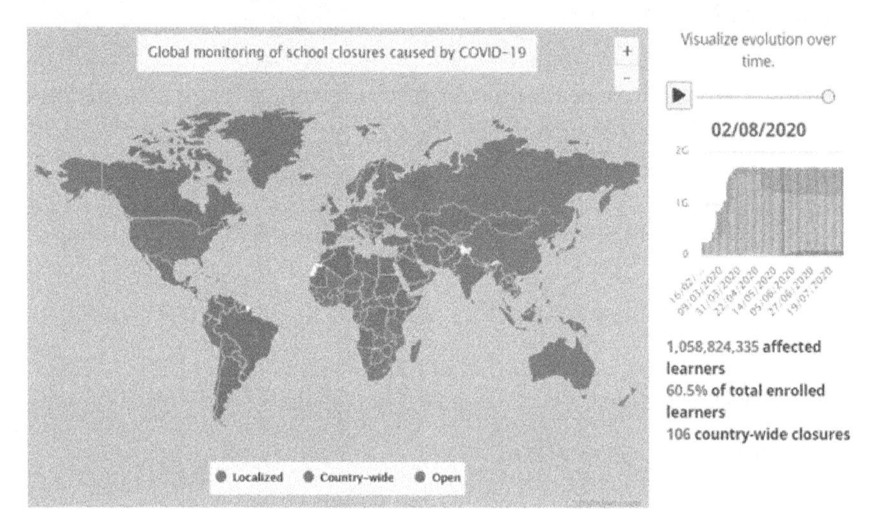

Figure 9 : Global monitoring of school closure (UNSECO accessed 22nd August 2020)

Note: Figures correspond to number of learners enrolled at pre-primary, primary, lower-secondary, and upper-secondary levels of education [ISCED levels 0 to 3], as well as at tertiary education levels [ISCED levels 5 to 8].

Internet Penetration in ASEAN Region:

The term "digital divide" has been used to define a gap in access to or use of internet devices. Digital exclusion in general reflects and entrenches broader patterns of disadvantage across age, gender, social and economic dimensions. As earlier mentioned, three countries have over 80% internet penetration, with Singapore leading the statistics, followed by Brunei and then Malaysia. For countries like Indonesia, the most populous nation in the region, have only 56%, with only 150 millions of its 268 million population having access to the internet. Thailand, Myanmar, and Vietnam also have less than 60% internet penetration, with 57%, 39%, 38% respectively in 2019 (Jalli, 2020). Chung et al. (2020) conducted a survey in Malaysia and found out that most preferred online learning via pre-recorded lectures were uploaded to Google Classroom and YouTube. In the ASEAN countries, many lecturers prefer to use different platforms, like Google Classroom or social media such as Facebook and YouTube. It could be because there is a huge digital divide among lecturers of different age groups (Shafie, Abd Majid & Ismail, 2019; Yaakob, Wan Hassan & Daud, 2016). While the biggest challenge for degree students is internet connectivity, for diploma students, it is the difficulty in understanding the content of the subject. According to Chung et al., (2020), the learners face eight main challenges during online education:

1. Internet connectivity
2. Too many different online learning methods used by different lecturers
3. Limited broadband data
4. Slow personal laptop and devices
5. Difficulty to focus due to distractions from the surroundings
6. Lack of motivation due to absence of face-to-face contact with friends and lecturers
7. Difficulty to understand the contents of the subjects
8. Lack of technical skills in using online learning

Moving forward, government telecommunication companies and universities should invest in developing internet infrastructure across the country as online learning will be the new norm in the foreseeable future. Universities also need to provide further training to enhance academic online teaching skills.

Education Sector Beyond Normal School

There are learners outside of the formal school system who are in dire need of urgent learning support. Some of them are low-skilled adults, women, out-of-school youth, migrants and refugees, and persons with disabilities.

Others are those who have suffered disproportionally from the suspension of face-to-face learning at the majority of adult learning centres and non-formal educational institutions.

Mental Health Concern

Press et al. (2020) studied that patients who are hospitalized cannot use inhalers correctly. Thus, virtual education improved the percentage of participants with correct technique compared with in-person education. The barriers patients face in using online health information and other health information technology may be more related to online capabilities rather than to technology access (Vollbrecht et al., 2020). Internet-based cognitive behaviour therapy (ICBT) can be effective in mental and somatic health care and usability correlated moderately negatively with age and moderately positively with digital health literacy skills but not with educational level (Rosalie van der Vaart et al 2019). Lin et al. (2016) found out that there is a positive association in the usage of social media and depression. Older adolescents who used social media passively by solely viewing content reported declines in well-being and life satisfaction, whereas those who used social media actively by interacting with others and posting content did not experience these declines (Kross et al. 2013). Another study found that teenagers who used Instagram to follow strangers and engage in social comparisons had higher depression symptoms, but others who followed friends and engaged in less social comparison had fewer depression symptoms (Lup et al., 2015). So, there is some specific concern when using social media. And while using online education, the social media use is inevitable.

Privacy Protection

Personal data privacy and protection is part of human rights as declared in Resolution 68/167 adopted by the United Nations (UN) General Assembly. This resolution emphasizes "unlawful or arbitrary surveillance and/or interception of communications, as well as unlawful or arbitrary collection of personal data, as highly intrusive acts, violate the rights to privacy and to freedom of expression." In this context, personal data of school students, most of whom are children, demand particular attention and more accurate measures. More and more countries and regions are adopting comprehensive regulations on personal data privacy and protection with regard to students and teachers.

Economic Setback

Global school closure generated an economic loss of $10 trillion. World estimated a loss of 16 percent of the investments that governments make in the basic education of this cohort of students. This is substantial setback in achieving the goal by 2030 unless drastic remedial action is taken (Azevedo et al., 2020).

> *When we are no longer able to change a situation - we are challenged to change ourselves.*
>
> *--Viktor E. Frankl*

Conclusion

With the current coronavirus (COVID-19) pandemic, many educational institutions especially higher education in most countries, including Southeast Asia, have transitioned to online learning. However, it has been challenging for students without access to the internet, and these digital inequalities persist across all countries. The study argues that the unexpected change to online teaching raised concerns in the formal learning milieu in Southeast Asia. Even though the world has become hyper-connected and internet penetration continues to increase every year, a large section of the population in Southeast Asia doesn't have access to the internet and electronic devices as many students are from economically vulnerable families. Even when different tries are made to implement online education through online platform, it is difficult to fully implement in the areas of sports, physical education and games like football especially in the absence of the social custom group activity. This could lead to different worries like mental health and thereby physical stress problems. In a nutshell, the feasibility challenges or hurdles are more than traditional teaching. But we are forced to adopt the new learning strategies and should refrain from looking more at the disadvantages and accept the changes. To achieve this end, education systems must confront issues of inequity front and centre. They must also prepare multi-modal responses, capitalizing on existing infrastructure and utilizing a combination of different learning mediums to ensure students are engaged and learning. The implementation of blended learning possibilities should be explored to a much extent to cope with the New "Normal" era.

References

Aguilar, J. (2012). Blended learning and the language teacher: A literature review. *Colombian Applied Linguistics Journal, 14*(2), 163–180.

Azevedo, J.P., Hasan, A., Goldemberg, D., Iqbal, S.A. and Geven, K., 2020. Simulating the potential impacts of covid-19 school closures on schooling and learning outcomes: A set of global estimates.

Chung, E., Subramaniam, G. and Dass, L.C., 2020. Online Learning Readiness Among University Students in Malaysia Amidst Covid-19. *Asian Journal of University Education*, *16*(2), pp.45-58. https://doi.org/10.24191/ajue.v16i2.10294.

Elliott, S. N., Kratochwill, T. R., Cook, J. L. and Travers, J. F. 2000. Educational Psychology: Effective Teaching, Effective Learning. New York, McGraw-Hill.

Gaol, F.L. and Hutagalung, F., 2020. The trends of blended learning in South East Asia. *Education and Information Technologies*, *25*(2), pp.659-663.

Gutman, L.M. 2013. The Impact of Non-cognitive Skills on Outcomes for Young People: Literature Review. London, Institute of Education. http://educationendowmentfoundation.org.uk/uploads/pdf/Non-cognitive_skills_literature_review.pdf (Accessed 19 February 2015.)

Hargis, J. 2001. Can students learn science using the internet? Journal of Research on Technology in Education, Vol. 33, No. 4, pp. 475–84

ITU (2019) https://www.itu.int/en/mediacentre/backgrounders/Pages/digital-inclusion-of-all.aspx. Accessed on 22nd August 2020.

Janicki, T. and Liegle, J. O. 2001. Development and evaluation of a framework for creating web-based learning modules: a pedagogical and systems perspective. Journal of Asynchronous Learning Networks, Vol. 5, No. 1, pp. 58–83

Kross, E., Verduyn, P., Demiralp, E., Park, J., Lee, D.S., Lin, N., Shablack, H., Jonides, J. and Ybarra, O., 2013. Facebook use predicts declines in subjective well-being in young adults. *PloS one*, *8*(8), p. e69841.

LAW, H.F.E. and MIURA, U., 2015. *Transforming teaching and learning in Asia and the Pacific: Case studies from seven countries.* UNESCO Bangkok Office. ISBN 978-92-9223-517-8 (print), 978-92-9223-518-5 (electronic)

Law, N. 2006. Leveraging technology for educational reform and pedagogical innovation: policies and practices in Hong Kong and Singapore. Research and Practice in Technology Enhanced Learning, Vol. 1, No. 2, pp. 163–70.

Lin, L.Y., Sidani, J.E., Shensa, A., Radovic, A., Miller, E., Colditz, J.B., Hoffman, B.L., Giles, L.M. and Primack, B.A., 2016. Association between social media use and depression among US young adults. *Depression and anxiety, 33*(4), pp.323-331.

Lo Bianco, J. (2010). Language policy and planning. In. N.H. Hornberger& S.L. McKay (Eds.), *Sociolinguistics and language education* (pp. 143–174).

Lup, K., Trub, L. and Rosenthal, L., 2015. Instagram# instasad? exploring associations among instagram use, depressive symptoms, negative social comparison, and strangers followed. *Cyberpsychology, Behavior, and Social Networking, 18*(5), pp.247-252.

Harris, S. 2002. Innovative pedagogical practices using ICT in schools in England. Journal of Computer Assisted Learning, Vol. 18, No. 4. pp. 449–58

Martinez-Garcia, A., Morris, S., Tscholl, M., Tracy, F. and Carmichael, P. 2012. Case-based learning, pedagogical innovation, and semantic web technologies. IEEE Transactions on Learning Technologies, Vol. 5, No. 2, pp. 104–16.

Mioduser, D., Nachmias, R., Tubin, D. and Forkosh-Baruch, A. 2003. Analysis schema for the study of domains and levels of pedagogical innovation in schools using ICT. Education and Information Technologies, Vol. 8, No. 1, pp. 23–36.

Jalli Nuurrianti (2020) Lack of internet access in Southeast Asia poses challenges for students to study online amid COVID-19 pandemic March 17, 2020 6.18pm AEDT

Olson, J., James, E. and Lang, M. 1999. Changing the subject: the challenge of innovation to teacher professionalism in OECD countries. Journal of Curriculum Studies, Vol. 31, No. 1, pp. 69–82.

Press VG, Arora VM, Kelly CA, Carey KA, White SR, Wan W. Effectiveness of Virtual vs In-Person Inhaler Education for Hospitalized Patients with Obstructive Lung Disease: A Randomized Clinical Trial. *JAMA Netw Open.* 2020;3(1): e1918205. Published 2020 Jan 3. doi:10.1001/jamanetworkopen.2019.18205. Retrieved from https://theconversation.com/lack-of-internet-access-in-southeast-asia-poses-challenges-for-students-to-study-online-amid-covid-19-pandemic-133787.

Rosen, J. A., Glennie, E. J., Dalton B. W., Lennon, J. M., and Bozick, R. N. 2010. Non-cognitive Skills in the Classroom: New Perspectives on Educational Research. RTI Press publication No. BK-0004-1009. Research Triangle Park, NC, RTI International. http://www.rti.org/rtipress. Accessed 11 December 2014.

Shafie, H., Abd Majid, F., Ismail, I.S. (2019) Technological Pedagogical Content Knowledge (TPACK) in Teaching 21st Century Skills in the 21st Century Classroom. Asian Journal of University Education, 15(3), 24-33.

Van der Vaart R, van Driel D, Pronk K, et al. The Role of Age, Education, and Digital Health Literacy in the Usability of Internet-Based Cognitive Behavioral Therapy for Chronic Pain: Mixed Methods Study. *JMIR Form Res*. 2019;3(4): e12883. Published 2019 Nov 21. doi:10.2196/12883.

Vollbrecht H, Arora V, Otero S, Carey K, Meltzer D, Press VG. Evaluating the Need to Address Digital Literacy Among Hospitalized Patients: Cross-Sectional Observational Study. *J Med Internet Res*. 2020;22 (6): e17519. Published 2020 Jun 4. doi:10.2196/17519.

Wu, J., Tennyson, R. D., Hsia, T. and Liao, Y. 2008. Analysis of e-learning innovation and core capability using a hypercube model. Computers in Human Behavior, Vol. 24, No. 5, pp. 1851–866.

Yaakob, H., Wan Hassan. W.H., Daud, S. (2016). Digital divide among elderly workers –a comparative study between public and private sectors in Melaka. Asian Journal of University Education.12(1), 53-82.

UNSECO (2020) https://en.unesco.org/covid19/educationresponse

8

Education During Covid-19 Crisis: Indian Perspective

Ajey Lele

Abstract

Covid-19 crisis has impacted every sphere of life. In the education sector, it is found reshaping existing teaching perspectives and practices. The world has witnessed major disruption in the traditional teaching practices. This 'new normal of the education' is anything but usual. Online learning has brought a revolution in the teaching methodologies. On the brighter side, it could be said that the Covid-19 disruption has opened gates for various new possibilities in reviving our education system. For many years the methods of distance education are in use in various parts of the world. However, the on-going pandemic crisis has advanced this form of education manifolds by using information technology-based tools. Earlier, the distance education used to happen more in form of as an education by correspondence. But now it is actually happening in real-time and not only for one individual, but in the form of virtual classrooms with many students attending simultaneously. However, online education has its own limitations and should not be viewed as a permanent solution.

Introduction

The coronavirus pandemic (Covid-19) has transformed the entire system of imparting education globally. Apart from the medical and pharmaceutical fraternity, it was the education fraternity which has responded very quickly to the growing crisis of Covid-19. The World Health Organization (WHO) announced COVID-19 as a global health crisis an outbreak of a pandemic on 11 March 2020. In fact, few weeks before the WHO announcing coronavirus disease as a pandemic many educational institutes in the world had already started using various new methodologies to reach to the students and impart education. This chapter broadly analyses the impact of COVID-19 crisis on the education system and their response. It also attempts to trace back the history of using the distance form of education.

Distance Education and Correspondence Courses

Distance education is defined as the practice of using correspondence, either written or virtual, to learn. With this practice, a teacher in one part of the world could provide training to students in different countries. This helps students contact teachers who may live geographically too far away to attend a class; it also assists students who cannot take classes during regular hours. Normally, this form of education has association with the adult education since mostly such students work for their livelihood and also could have some other responsibilities.

The exact origins of distance education are under debate and there could be different views on this subject. But, known earliest modern form could be traced back to Europe in the early 1800s. The initial courses were pre-designed materials that would be mailed through the postal service to learners who couldn't join universities either because of geography or the high cost of tuition or their inability to attend courses during regular time. Normally, this form of education was referred as correspondence education (Study.Com 2003-2020). Such form of education lacked the personal touch since there were no face to face meetings with the teachers and fellow students. Also, owing to the mindset of society at large, the individuals undertaking correspondence courses were not rated highly in regards to the standard of their education in some parts of the world.

By the late 1800s, correspondence courses had started establishing its roots in the United States (US). Various colleges and universities began offering correspondence courses, including some of the large schools, such as Baylor University and the University of Chicago. Slowly, the acceptance in distance education grew leading to an increase in the number of schools offering this form of education. By the mid-1900s, educational institutions all around the world started relying on correspondence courses to complement their on-campus studies (Study.Com 2003-2020).

Digital Platforms: Revolutionising Distance Education

Over a period of time with advancements in technologies, particularly in the of Information Technologies (IT) and owing to the growth in Internet the nature of distance learning has much evolved. This different form of distance education started getting recognised as e-learning, and online learning. Here the system of imparting education has remained same and that is the physical separation of teachers and students all through teaching. But, the most significant change in this form of education than the earlier form of distance education is that the students and teachers are able to commutate in real-time via audio and/or video link. Obviously, the direct and real-time form of communication improves the quality of learning. All this bring forward the vast difference between correspondence training and on-line training. Distance learning customarily has focused on non-traditional students, such as full-time workers, military personnel, people who cannot afford fulltime residential education and non-residents or individuals in remote regions who are unable to attend classroom lectures. However, distance learning has become a recognised part of the educational system, with trends pointing to ongoing growth. More than a decade back in the US alone, more than 5.6 million university students were enrolled in at least one online course in the autumn of 2009, up from 1.6 million in 2002.

Currently, an increasing number of universities are found providing various distance learning opportunities. A pioneer in the field is the University of Phoenix (Arizona, 1976) and by the first decade of the 21st century had become the largest private school in the world, with more than 400,000 enrolled students. It was one of the earliest adopters of distance learning technology, although many of its students spend some time in classrooms on one of its dozens of campuses in the United States, Canada, and Puerto Rico (Michael Simonson and Gary A. Berg. 2016). Actually, more than the developed world, it is the developing world that required investments in open and distance education systems. One of the early realisers of this system is the country like India which has established the Indira Gandhi National Open University, New Delhi, while China has the China Central Radio and TV University at Beijing.

The Indira Gandhi National Open University (IGNOU), got established by an Act of Parliament in 1985 in India. It has continuously striven to build an inclusive knowledge society through inclusive education. The university began by offering two academic programmes in 1987, i.e., Diploma in Management and Diploma in Distance Education, with a strength of 4,528 students (Indira Gandhi National Open University. 2014). Today, IGNOU has more than 20 schools and many centres. It has developed a major network within the country and also in more than 15 other countries. The university is probably catering for more than 4 million students presently. While less than a decade before India, the open university of China got established in Beijing in 1979. This university is directly under the supervision of the Ministry of Education.

Apart from universities, there are also few non-governmental organisations (NGOs) which are significantly contributing to improving that quality and expanse of the distance education. The United States Distance Learning Association (USDLA) is the first non-profit distance learning association in the US established during 1987 to support distance learning research, development and praxis across the complete arena of education, training and communications. The organisation was established with a view to impart learning via new concepts of the fusion of communication technologies with learning in broad multi-discipline applications (United States Distance Learning Association 2020).

For many years now, the modern distance learning courses are known to employ Web-based course-management systems that incorporate digital reading materials, podcasts (recorded sessions for electronic listening or viewing at the student's leisure), e-mail, threaded (linked) discussion forums, chat rooms, and test-taking functionality in virtual (computer-simulated) classrooms. This modern form of learning is known to be allowing students to access live video and audio educational content. They get shared access to electronic documents at scheduled times. Shared social spaces in the form of blogs and collaboratively edited documents. The advent of Massive Open Online Courses (MOOCs) in the first and second decades of the 21st century characterised a major shift in direction for distance learning (Gary A. Berg &Michael Simonson 2016). It is important to review the post Covid-19 form of education against this backdrop. The progress made in the forms of distant education since 19th century onwards definitely has helped the people in the form of an already available templet.

Web-based education was a time-tested and a successful model available for various educational agencies to bank upon. Hence, various modern ways of teaching is introduced in the post Covid-19 are actually juxta-positioning of new methodologies on an old platform.

Education during Pandemic

Major health related crises are found ongoing since December 2019 in India. It all began in China and within six months it ended up influencing almost the entire world. The outbreak of coronavirus disease (COVID-19) has been declared a Public Health Emergency of International Concern (PHEIC). Even by end of August 2020 a lot was unknown about the virus that causes COVID-19, still now it is not that clear if it gets transmitted through direct contact with respiratory droplets of an infected person (generated through coughing and sneezing), as individuals can also be infected from touching surfaces contaminated with the virus and touching their face (e.g., eyes, nose, mouth) (UNICEF 2020). There have been some claims by Russia in regards to the discovery of a vaccine for this disease (Sputnik V) however, it is not yet clear that how effective it is and if it would take some more months for a reliable vaccine to be available. Owing to this pandemic crisis the biggest suffering happened in the education sector along with the economic sector. Obviously, the view was that just because there is a social distancing rule and students are expected not to leave home that does not mean that education should stop. First, there was a thinking that schools and universities can run with proper preventative mechanisms in place. All this forced the school administrations to find the best solutions under the present crisis. There was also an economic element associated with it since in some parts of the world parents started claiming that they would not like to pay the fees since schools were kept closed. Since, there were job losses happening at the same time many parents were found losing their own jobs and were not in position to pay the fees of their children. Schools also faced difficulties, they were also not in a position to pay to their teachers and other staffs regularly. All these issues and concerns also initiated the on-line education in India. Also, it is important to mention that already there was a model available about the distance education and that was followed by most of the educational Institutions in India.

Broadly, professionals have observed that there could be 3 ways the coronavirus pandemic could reshape education:

1. The coronavirus pandemic has changed how millions around the globe are educated.
2. New solutions for education could bring much needed innovation.
3. Given the digital divide, new shifts in education approaches could widen equality gaps (Gloria Tam & Diana El-Azar 2020).

In few weeks' time, coronavirus (COVID-19) has changed how students should be educated around the world. The spread of virus seems to have happened with phenomenal speed. Very rapidly, it has covered all continents and regions: from Asia, Europe, the Middle East, and the United States. After the announcement by WHO about this disease being a pandemic many countries have taken swift and decisive actions to mitigate the development of a full-blown pandemic. Since February/ March 2020 it got decided that suspending attendance at schools and universities would help the administration to implement the preventative mechanism more swiftly. Also, probably at the political level there was a realisation that anything owing wrong with the health of the younger generation owing to coronavirus could emerge as a major setback to the state's administration. All this led to taking extreme precautions at various levels. As of 13 March, the Organisation for Economic Co-operation and Development (OECD) estimated that over 421 million children were affected due to school closures announced or implemented in 39 countries. Around the same time, another 22 countries had announced partial "localised" closures.

Such risk-control decisions have led millions of students into temporary 'home-schooling' situations, especially in some of the most heavily impacted countries like South Korea, Italy, Iran. During the same time India, also turned towards the home schools. There is a flip side to any such decision making. Such systematic changes have also caused a degree of inconvenience, but they have also driven new examples of educational innovation. Though it is too early to judge how reactions to COVID-19 will affect the global education systems, there are indications that it could have a long-term impact on the trajectory of learning innovation and digitisation (Gloria Tam & Diana El-Azar 2020).

Actually, using technology in education is not a new idea. Educators are always motivated to personalise learning for students; technology can help them significantly. For last few decades technology is known to be transforming education, changing how, when and where students learn, and empowering them at every stage of their journey. There are various models available which help in personalising learning. It is a well-established fact that technology empowers students by giving them ownership of how they learn, making education relevant to their lives and preparing them for their futures. Through technology and access to resources beyond classrooms, students do get inspired to become problem-solvers, critical thinkers, collaborators, and creators. In various schools the technology has been successfully integrated into classrooms, students develop a lifelong love of learning (Intel. n.d). However, there is a subtle difference between the use of technology in education during the Covid-19 time and pre Covid-19 time. Before the world getting into the grip of present pandemic, technology was used as a 'multiplier' in education. It was an aid for the teacher to enhance the classroom training. However, during the Covid-19 time the technology has emerged as a platform to impart training. E-learning as becoming as an alternative to the class-room learning.

It is said that use of technology in teaching improves the engagement of the students. Even online learning could be a fun and bring in lot amount of enjoyment. Immediately after Covid-19 crisis began, the teacher community (not all) is known to have got caught in the zone which they were not comfortable for teaching. Also, the student community was finding it difficult to adopt to this new method of teaching. In some part of the world actually, the e-learning was happening but that was basically for the community which was undertaking classes under the distance education programme. However, for the students, particularly studying in primary schools, this was an altogether new experience. Also, they normally do not have the patience to sit and study in front of the computer screen. More so studying in the atmosphere of own home with parents around was an entirely different experience. It has been found that the students studying in the higher classes have quickly adopted to this new form of learning. In fact, many of them were also using various software-based tools for learning during their non-school hours and hence got used to the new system.

The COVID-19 pandemic has exacerbated inequalities in education systems across the world. According to a recent UNESCO report, about 40% of low- and lower-middle-income countries have not supported learners at risk of exclusion during this crisis, such as the poor, linguistic minorities and learners with disabilities. The 2020, the Global Education Monitoring Report (GEMR) noted that efforts to maintain continuity in learning during the pandemic may have actually worsened exclusion trends. During the height of school closures in April 2020, almost 91% of students around the world were out of school. The report also emphasis that education systems responded with distance learning solutions, all of which offered less or more imperfect substitutes for classroom instruction. It has been also noted that many poor countries have opted for radio and television lessons, 55% of low-income, 73% of lower-middle-income and 93% of upper-middle-income countries adopted for online learning platforms for primary and secondary education (The Hindu 2020).

India and Education in Covid-19 Era

At a regional level a mix picture emerges both that of some success and some failure in respect of imparting education during the present crisis. It would be interesting to have a look at a case of India in this regard. The democratic India is one of the developed countries in the Asian region and is a known IT powerhouse. There is a reasonable internet cover at least in some parts of the country. Also, there have been some programmes which indicates that efforts are been done to increase the internet connectivity even to the remote villages. There are programmes like 'Internet Saathi' (Internet friend) programme. This was launched as a pilot project in 2015. This 'Internet Saathi' programme focuses on educating women how to use the Internet, who then impart training to other women in their community and neighbouring villages. Google's 'Internet Saathis' now covers 2.6 lakh Indian villages (Surabhi Agarwal 2017). It is expected that if a mother is trained then obviously the children would also get the teachings and knowledge from their mother. It is not known the exact impact of this programme. However, possibly it could have helped the mothers to help their small children to undertake e-teaching.

India's multi-layered society mandates a strong public education system integrating a holistic vision. Owing to the size of the country, huge population, cast system, it has not been possible for the country to evolve a discrimination-free education system. Now, this current pandemic has magnified disparities like never before. For country like India lockdowns to contain the spread of the COVID-19 pandemic have posed many challenges for school education. It is known to have impacted the children's education, particularly of those from marginalised sections. There has been much of a physiological impact on the minds of the students. Particularly, it appears that the children in rural India could be the major sufferers of this new convention called 'study from home'. There are some informal inputs available indicating that some of such children are been asked by their parents to help them in the work in agricultural fields. Some earlier reports indicate that India has around 1.4 million schools, 2.01 million children enrolled in government schools from Standard 1-8 and an additional 3.8 million children enrolled in Standard 9-10. Approximately 29% of India's population are children, and 19.29 % is in the age group of 6-14 years. This group is legally entitled to education under the Right to Education (RTE) Act, 2009 (Aparajita Sharma. (2020). However, the present-day learning platforms like desktop computers, laptops and mobile telephones are not available with many students form economically weaker sections or people from rural areas.

The broad observation based on informal talks with the teacher community in India indicates that India's online education system during Covid-19 crisis is a partial success. Mainly in the metropolitan cities where good facilities towards private schooling are available e-learning is found taking its roots and mainly for higher classes the response from students is good. Not going to the school is also saving lot of time of the students. This is allowing them put in additional efforts towards preparing for the competitive examinations. However, the overall learning system is known to be working adequately for the students whose parents are from middle and high-income group. But many times, even these students are finding some difficulties in the learning since there is no face to face contact with their teachers and classmates.

There are major challenges in regards to the working in laboratories to perform experiments. This problem is mainly for the subjects belonging to the science stream. Alternative solutions like virtual laboratories and communicating simulations are used for practical assessments. Teachers are found learning to make animations and small films/ videos for better explanation of both theory and particles. They allow the students to perform experiments, collect data and answer questions to assess their understanding.

Conclusion

All in all, present-day methods (e-teaching) of imparting education outside the school/collage complexes is a temporary option and all credit should be given to the teaching and students community for finding a viable alternative in the time of crisis. However, it needs to be understood that learning in school premises is not only about classroom teaching, it is the environment in which the growth of a child happens. Let us hope that we find a permanent solution to the ongoing Covid-19 crisis and the children would be able to go back to the schools/collages which are actually the temples for their overall development as human-beings.

References

Aparajita Sharma. (2020). COVID-19 Lockdown Lessons and the Need to Reconsider Draft New Education Policy. The Wire. https://thewire.in/education/covid-19-lockdown-lessons-and-the-need-to-reconsider-draft-new-education-policy, accessed on 11 August, 2020

Gary A. Berg &Michael Simonson, (2016) "Distance learning", https://www.britannica.com/topic/distance-learning/Academic-issues-and-future-directions, accessed on 1 August, 2020

Gary A. Berg, "Distance learning", https://www.britannica.com/topic/distance-learning/Academic-issues-and-future-directions, accessed on 1 August, 2020

Gloria Tam & Diana El-Azar (2020). Global Agenda:3 ways the coronavirus pandemic could reshape educationhttps://www.weforum.org/agenda/2020/03/3-ways-coronavirus-is-reshaping-education-and-what-changes-might-be-here-to-stay/, accessed on 10 July, 2020

Indira Gandhi National Open University. 2014. Preamble. http://www.ignou.ac.in/ignou/aboutignou/profile/2, accessed on 16 August, 2020

Gloria Tam & Diana El-Azar (2020). Global Agenda:3 ways the coronavirus pandemic could reshape educationhttps://www.weforum.org/agenda/ 2020/03/3-ways-coronavirus-is-reshaping-education-and-what-changes-might-be-here-to-stay/, accessed on 10 July, 2020

Intel. (n.d). Use of Technology in Education for Learning and Teaching: A 360^0 Approach to Student Success. https://www.intel.in/content/www/in/en/education/technology-in-education-for-learning-and-teaching.html, accessed on 16 August, 2020

Study.Com. (2003-2020). What Is Distance Education? - Definition & History. https://study.com/academy/lesson/what-is-distance-education-definition-history.html, accessed on 7 August, 2020

Study.Com. (2003-2020). What Is Distance Education? - Definition & History. https://study.com/academy/lesson/what-is-distance-education-definition-history.html, accessed on 7 August, 2020

Surabhi Agarwal. (2017). Google's Internet Saathi programme reaches 100,000 villages. The Economic Times. https://economictimes.indiatimes.com/tech/internet/googles-internet-saathi-programme-reaches-100000-villages/articleshow/59883935.cms, accessed on 14 August, 2020.

The Hindu. (2020). Coronavirus lockdown | COVID-19 widened educational divide: UNESCO report. https://www.thehindu.com/education/coronavirus-lockdown-covid-19-widened-educational-divide-unesco-report/article31907857.ece, accessed on 12 August, 2020

UNICEF. (2020). Key Messages and Actions for COVID-19 Prevention and Control in Schools. https://www.who.int/docs/default-source/coronaviruse/key-messages-and-actions-for-covid-19-prevention-and-control-in-schools-march-2020.pdf?sfvrsn=baf81d52_4&download=true.

United States Distance Learning Association. (2020). History. https://usdla.org/about/history/, accessed on 28 July 2020

9

Impact of COVID-19 on Russian Society and on the Education System

Nivedita Das Kundu

Abstract

The COVID-19 pandemic, lockdown and self-isolation have changed many things around the world and the same is found happening in Russia too. The Chapter examines the impact of COVID-19 on the Russian society with emphasis on the education sector. The study argues that COVID-19 disrupted the education system in schools, colleges and universities and the educational institutions were closed in an attempt to contain the spread of the virus. Schools were forced to replace the compulsory face-to-face in class education with online learning and home schooling helped by both teachers and parents. The study reveals that students and teachers adapted to the online education system and were obliged to follow the distance learning. However, there have been challenges adjusting to these changes for students, teachers and the parents. Also, the pressure on the medical infrastructure is increasing. The health sector is finding it difficult to manage both professionals as well as, the administrative aspects of handling the overall load on the medical system. Conceivably, the initial reluctance of the administration to recognise the possible enormity of the threat is probably responsible for their medical system's failure in some parts of Russia. Owing to the massive influx of patients, the inadequacies of social support became evident and healthcare sectors were and are found to be increasingly overwhelmed. The COVID-19 pandemic has taught

Russians that access to healthcare and medication is of utmost importance for the survival of the state itself. Only time will tell if there is a necessity to change the lifestyle, overall teaching and learning process and upgrade the technology.

Introduction

The outbreak of the COVID-19 pandemic in Russia from the middle of March 2020 affected the population with unexpected disruptions in almost all spheres of life and drastically altered the lifestyle of the Russian population. The lockdown announced on 29 March 2020 to contain the infection and slow down the spread of the virus was an extraordinary decision taken by the Russian government in post-Soviet history (Institute Montaigne, 2020). The COVID-19 crisis reached Russia when Kremlin was busy focusing its political decisions to push for the constitutional amendments for allowing Vladimir Putin to stay in power after 2024. However, as the coronavirus cases started increasing, the Russian government hurriedly declared lockdown measures and asked citizens to stay at home and maintain physical distancing.

Russia's response to the coronavirus outbreak started much earlier and Russia was quick in deciding to close its borders of about 2,615 km long with China. On 27 January 2020, Russia also created special coronavirus headquarters. However, on 31 January, two Russian regions announced that two Chinese tourists carried the virus, making them the first confirmed cases in Russia. Chinese tourists were temporarily banned from entering in Russian cities from 20 February 2020. But the closing of borders raised many other related problems and therefore, the border had to partially reopen (Mahmood, 2020). The Russian government was active in controlling the cases in January and February as the situation was still under control and the number of virus cases was much lower. But things changed fast and confirmed cases gradually spiked up and looking into the situation, the Russian government had to announce the strict quarantine orders.

Russia rapidly climbed up the global COVID-19 ladder in May 2020, reaching third place globally after the COVID-19 case numbers in Brazil overtook Russia. According to data compiled by John Hopkins University, by the end of May, the daily incidence figures appeared to have plateaued in Russia. Russia gradually overtook the cases in France and Germany.

More than half of Russia's COVID-19 cases were found in big crowded cities like Moscow and St. Petersburg thus making the healthcare system in these cites overwhelmed. Reports of extreme stress in Russian health care sector personnel's physical and mental health issues also came up. The chapter tries to examine the impact of the COVID-19 in Russian societies, in the education sectors, focussing on the pandemic measures taken by the administration for continuing the regular life, at the same time, protecting the citizens from the deadly virus.

Socio-Political Impact

The COVID-19 affected a huge number of people in Russia and within a short time, the pandemic made Russians change their daily routine. Though Russia has good experience in controlling infectious diseases and disease like plagues, but within a short period, the threat of COVID-19 became much more dangerous than any other threats. However, the disruptions in normal life became evident as educational institutions were closed, almost all the entire sectors of the economy closed down. At the same time, along with the COVID-19 health crisis, the economic crisis deepened too in Russia. The pandemic has pushed many into poverty and many-faced difficulties in storing food and paying their bills. To manage the pandemic and at the same time, implement mechanisms to successfully rescue the economy became quite difficult for Russia.

President Putin connected with a number of world leaders and discussed the need for cooperation in dealing with COVID-19. The 75th Anniversary of the allied victory in the Second World War was another significant context to connect with the global leaders during the same time. United States of America's President Donald Trump offered to send ventilators to Russia, returning the favour of the Russian assistance in April 2020. Presidents Putin and XI Jinping appreciated the two-way cooperation as Russia had sent medical equipment when the infection in China was at its peak. Thereafter, Russia has been importing personal protective equipment (PPE) from China to supplement Russia's daily production of about 9 million masks. Vietnam, which has one of the most remarkable records of dealing with COVID-19, continued the assistance in this tough time (Gorvachev Foundation Research Report, 2020). However, Russia promised to support its neighbouring Central Asian countries of

Kazakhstan, Uzbekistan and Tajikistan with medical supply to cope up with the difficulties during the pandemic.

Virus Escalation Factors

Many factors played in the case of Russia's increase in COVID-19 infections. Like in many other countries, in Russia, the health care sectors also faced significant shortages with personal protective equipment (PPE). Russia's health care sector workers became more vulnerable due to PPE shortages (BBC NEWS, 2020). Also, the hospitals faced problems due to the shortages of ventilators. Above all, there were regional variations in the availability of PPE and ventilators. As such the quality of the health care system differs greatly across Russia's regions. This is because of varying levels of preparation and available equipment's. This differentiation caused problems with the overall public health system in Russia and in tackling the hardship caused during the pandemic (Rainsford, 2020). During the COVID-19 pandemic, many countries suffered due to the lack of clear political leadership. In the case of Russia too, it has been noted that the Russian President's response to the pandemic was not as per the requirement. He avoided handling the situation directly and refrained from addressing citizens regularly on how to tackle the crisis, which became routine affairs for many countries' leaders. (Deprez, 2020). Strong leadership in the face of the global pandemic was essential and that was missing in the case of Russia.

President Putin's popularity peaked up within the country immediately after Russia annexed Crimea. However, recent reports and interviews suggested that due to COVID-19 concerns, significant destruction has happened in his public support. Besides, the discontent among Russia's working population also grew up due to the fall in real wages, due to the rise in taxation and inefficient delivery of services. The economic pain caused due to COVID-19 and unhappiness about its handling by the Russian government seems to have caused damage to President Putin's popularity. (Raghavan, 2020).

For the last two decades in Russia, people relied on President Putin's direct intervention and control over any crisis situation. However, President Putin's intervention during the COVID-19 pandemic was considerably limited (The Lancet, 2020). His response to the pandemic was quite unusual for the centralized state power like Russia.

Pandemic Confusion and Measures

During the pandemic, the regional leaders in Russia were given the power to take-up decisions about their own region's safety and health measures. This was unusual for Russia and it was not clear if Kremlin would intervene if the regional leader's radical decisions failed. Also, it was not clear if decisions taken by the regional leaders would be approved by the Kremlin (The Lancet, 2020). However, one thing became clear that President Putin was unwilling to take charge of the pandemic crisis and therefore, the decision making process to tackle the crisis was shifted to the local leaders. This created confusion and people started struggling to adjust to the new normal.

On 11 May 2020, President Putin in his address to the Nation on the pandemic called an end to Russia's "non-working period". President Putin mentioned in the televised address to the nation that the pandemic and the lockdown had a strong impact on the economy of Russia and it affected millions of Russians. Therefore, the pandemic measures that have prevented workers from going to their work formally ended on 12 May in Russia, even though the COVID-19 cases increased considerably (Russia TV Report, 2020). However, many COVID-19 related health restrictions remained in place with a gradual easing to be carried out at different speeds in various regions of the country, depending on local developments.

Russian army medical personnel who had been sent to Italy to fight COVID-19 cases were asked to return to Russia to help to combat the increasing spread of the virus within Russia (The Moscow Times, 2020). During the lockdown period, many places in Russia especially some industrial establishments did not close down in total. Many manufacturing units outside the urban centres functioned as usual. However, Russia's overall industrial output shrank by about a quarter in April 2020 (as per Bloomberg estimates). The Russian government announced three packages of support for businesses and individuals. Half of it was in cash handouts, and the rest consisted of tax breaks or the waiving of obligatory payments. Nonetheless, as part of the lockdown measures in Russia, wages were paid by companies for furloughed workers, but many companies also refused to pay to their workers who did not return to work after the lockdown was called off. Nevertheless, the return to work for Russian workers clashed with various confusing messages from the regional leaders (Farngis & Lyubov 2020).

Russia announced that around 236,000 Russian citizens had been brought back to Russia from COVID-19 affected countries. However, many were still waiting to return to Russia. The Russian government extended the visa period for foreign nationals whose visas expired after 15 March. They were automatically extended to 15 September, 2020.

Pandemic Restriction Effect

Migrants labourers mainly from neighbouring countries of Central Asia engaged in Russia's agricultural and service sectors especially in physically demanding labour work. For instance, work at construction sites, farms, and factories. Seasonal vegetable and fruit farms suffered due to COVID-19 restrictions. This was mainly due to the border closing and lockdown. Russia's agricultural sector is highly dependent on neighbouring Central Asian workers to harvest their seasonal crops. The sector got affected due to the lockdown as thousands of migrant labourers from Central Asian countries were stopped from entering into Russia. This seriously affected the food supply chains. In order to reduce the difficulty in certain seasonal agricultural sectors, students and prisoners were recruited (Farngis & Lyubov, 2020), but such options did not work well.

Teaching and Learning during Pandemic

COVID-19 disrupted the education system in schools, colleges and universities in Russia. All the educational institutions were closed. Like in many other countries the Russian government also took the decision to close the schools in an attempt to contain the spread of the virus. Schools were forced to replace the compulsory face to face in class education with online learning and home schooling, helped by teachers and parents both (OECD, 2020). Due to the closedown of the educational institutions, students and teachers adapted to the online education system and were obliged to follow the distance learning. There have been challenges adjusting to these changes for students, teachers and parents. The COVID-19 crisis has changed the life of many students. Students and their families both started learning to operate under a condition of uncertainty and risk-prevention, which also affected students' academic motivation level. Students needed both the support of their parents and teachers to engage with their learning and reduce anxiety in the stressful time of COVID-19. In the Russian Federation, about 84% of students felt that their parents and their teachers both supported their efforts. Many universities in Russia changed from in class learning to distance learning and immediately granted free access to the study materials, attracting students to continue their learning process across Russia (Vermishev & Dmitriev, (2020). Students were allowed to take the online courses and pass the exams and receive credit from their own Universities.

The teachers monitored attendance regularly and check everyone's presence in the screenshot. Teachers started conveying information in the same way online as they used to do in the class lectures. Teachers also addressed the gaps of parents of young students who were struggling to learn how to navigate the online tools and assist their children. During the online teaching, students and teachers maintained continuous communication with one another, especially, through email or video communications. Students started communicating with their friends and classmates through social media portals and became used to this medium of communication. During the time of the pandemic people became more resilient.

Nonetheless, Russian children returned to school during the first week of September after six-months break. All necessary measures were taken by the school authorities and by local government to prevent COVID-19 outbreak among students or teachers. Mass testing of school employees, daily temperature checks and intensive handwashing for everyone became compulsory in schools in Russia. School timing changed for students to avoid gathering in bigger groups. Instead of students going to teachers, teachers started coming to students to avoid any possible cluster of students at one place. Many schools even installed sophisticated temperature screening devices near the front entrance door. As the children walk inside, cameras take their pictures and a thermometer scans their temperature and the results are displayed on a monitor for security staff (Cris, 2020). Russian President Putin addressed the nation through a teleconference call to address the back to school and significance of learning while maintaining the COVID-19 precautions.

Pandemic Treatment

The COVID-19 pandemic helped Russians to be more connected with their local community and local health care system. In all likelihood, the pandemic will stay for long. Russian scientists and researchers worked on almost 50 different vaccine projects. A drug called Avifavir received a temporary registration certificate from the Ministry of Health of the Russian Federation for treating COVID-19 patients during the initial stages. Health officials registered a second drug for a treatment called Levilimab (trade name Ilsira) (The Hindu, 2020). Russian media reports mentioned that at least seven research facilities were working on coronavirus vaccines. Two forms of vaccine developed by the Moscow based Gamalei National Research Center for Epidemiology and Microbiology in cooperation with the Russian Defence Ministry and Clinical Trials also took place. Both military and civilian personnel were asked to take the trials. The Russian Defence Ministry noted that the parameters for the sample of volunteers have been discussed with the Ministry of Health. The tests conducted on two groups of volunteers and volunteers were isolated in two Moscow hospitals for observation (Tickle, 2020). On 11 August, Russia announced that their COVID-19 vaccine is ready for registering as a first coronavirus vaccine and named the vaccine as Sputnik V. This name is chosen to revive memories of the Soviet Sputnik, being the first satellite in space. President Putin's daughter was claimed to be among the first to be inoculated as this is a long-standing Soviet tradition where researchers and public personalities volunteering to test newly-developed vaccines. Two weeks later, President Putin announced that his daughter was doing good and also safe after both doses of the vaccine taken by her. The Russian Defence Minister was also publicly shown taking the vaccine dosage.

However, there was a criticism by many international health organisations on this drastic move by Russia to register an untested vaccine. The phase 1 and 2 results of the vaccine were published in the reputed medical research journal *The Lancet*, claiming strong immune responses in all the 76 patients tested. It was reported that phase 3 trials had commenced, involving more than 40,000 people at over 45 medical centres around Russia. This makes it one of the nine vaccine candidates in late-stage trials as of date, as per world health organisation. Russian health officials announced that trials may also be conducted in India, UAE, Saudi Arabia and Philippines. Mass production already started and Russia claims a production capacity of 500 million doses per year (Raghavan, 2020).

Conclusion

There are various challenges from education to the environment, to economic and healthcare sector, that would require apt handling during the COVID-19 era. All these could lead to a fundamental restructuring of societies around the ideals of local self-sufficiency, improvised medical practices and environmental sustainability. There is a realisation that managing pandemics like this requires global support. No country can operate in isolation and there is a need for international collaboration. The leadership has to be upfront in managing the pandemic crisis and concerns. Russia has been active at multilateral fora's like the Shanghai Cooperation Organisation (SCO), Brazil, Russia, India, China and South Africa (BRICS) and in many other such forums, where the issue like pandemic can be discussed and joint efforts can be initiated. However, when it comes to agencies like the World Health Organisation (WHO), not much exuberance is visible and this needs to change by bigger nations like Russia. Thereby, Russia needs to be more proactive in its dealings with COVID-19 situation. Over the years President Putin has tried to project Russia's influence at the global level by leveraging military, political, economic and business ties with many countries. All in all, handling crisis is not new for Russia and surely, they would come out of this crisis as will the rest of the world in a few months' time. However, the dents caused due to the COVID-19 crisis in the education, healthcare, economic sectors, would take time to heal in Russia.

References

BBC News. (2020). Coronavirus: Russian hospital staff 'working without masks' https://www.bbc.co.uk/news/av/world-europe-52508834.

Cris, B. (2020). "Temperature checks and no masks: School is back in Russia, but classes look much the same." Available at https://www.cbc.ca/news/world/russia-school-resumes-precautions-covid-19-1.5710499.

Deprez, F. (2020). "Russia's Confusing Covid-19 Response." Available at

https://www.fpri.org/article/2020/04/russias-confusing-covid-19-response/. Accessed August 2020.

Farngis. N. & Lyubov C. (2020). "Covid19: Putin Ends Russia's 'Nonworking Period'; Kazakhstan Eases Restrictions." Available at https://www.rferl.org/a/covid-19-moscow-mortality-surge-death-toll-underreported/30605393.html.Accessed August 2020.

Farngis, N. & Lyubov, C. (2020). "Russian Farmers Suffering as Covid-19 Pandemic Keeps Central Asian Workers at Home." Available at https://www.rferl.org/a/russian-farmers-suffering-as-covid-19-pandemic-keeps-central-asian-workers-at-home/30652482.html.

Gorvachev Foundation Research Report. (2020). "Covid-19 and Russia's Response." April 2020.

Mahmood, B. (2020). "Russia is Now in the Top 5 Countries Most Affected by the Coronavirus", 5 August 2020. Available at https://www.newsweek.com/russia-covid-19-coronavirus-moscow-putin-1502737. Accessed August 2020.

Institut Montaigne. (2020). Is Covid-19 a Game-Changer for Russia? https://www.institutmontaigne.org/en/blog/covid-19-game-changer-russia. Accessed August 2020.

OECD. (2020). "School Education During Covid-19: Were Teachers and Students Ready?" Available at http://www.oecd.org/education/Russian-Federation-coronavirus-education-country-note.pdf.

Raghavan P.S. (2020). "Russia's Covid-19 Challenges Mount. *Ananta India Russia Review*. Vol 05, Issue 5.

Raghavan P.S. (2020). "Russia Report", *Ananta Aspen*.Vol.5, Issue 8.

Rainsford, S. (2020). Coronavirus: Russian republic Dagestan enduring a 'catastrophe'. https://www.bbc.com/news/world-europe-52737404. Accessed August 2020.

Russia TV Report, 11 May 2020.

The Lancet. (2020). "Salient lessons from Russia's COVID-19 outbreak." https://www.thelancet.com/pdfs/journals/lancet/PIIS0140-6736(20)31280-0.pdf.

The Hindu. (2020). "Russia to Roll Out Covid-19 Drug Next Week." Available at

https://www.thehindu.com/news/international/russia-to-roll-out-covid-19-drug-next-week/article31725174.ece

The Moscow Times. (2020). "Health Workers' Risk of Death from Covid-19." Available at https://www.themoscowtimes. com/2020/05/19/russian- medics-16x-more-likely-to-die-from-coronavirus-than-foreign-colleagues-analysis-a70311. Accessed August 2020.

Tickle. J. (2020). "Light at the end of the tunnel? Russian Scientists Test Potential Covid-19 Vaccine on 18 Volunteers." Available at https://www.rt.com/russia/492252-russian-scientists-covid19-vaccine-tested/

Vermishev, G. & Dmitriev, D. (2020). "Distance Learning: The Pandemic's Effects on Russian Education." Available at https://sras.org/pandemic-effects-russian-education/. Accessed August 2020.

10

Interactions between Teachers and Students in online Learning during COVID-19 Crisis in Egypt

Taghreed ElGhandour

Abstract

Education plays an essential role in an individual's life. It is through this process that people initially formulate and reformulate their thoughts with the help and guidance of the instructors within the boundaries of educational institutions. Parallel to this phenomenon, individuals are able to discover their strengths as well as apply them to practical life. In this repute, it is important to utilize all aspects of the learning process, including online procedures of teaching and learning that are so important in today's world. A shift to online education truly requires huge adjustments. There may be an increase in the relationship between student's actual interactions and participation, as well as their learning performance. These are considerable grounds for rejecting our traditional mode of teaching/ learning and taking huge steps towards online education. The COVID-19 pandemic has led to mass school and university closures worldwide. Egypt is no different and the impact on the country's education sector has been overwhelming. The Chapter argues that school closures due to the COVID-19 pandemic affected students as well as, teachers and that the COVID-19 revealed globally the opportunities and constraints of using Education Technology (EdTech). The study reveals that in the absence of face-to-face teaching and learning, Egyptian schools and universities created platforms where teachers could host lesson plans. As a result, a wide range of open educational resources were freely available to students, enabling approximately 22 million students distributed over 55,000 schools to communicate with teachers. On the flipside, there were limitations. There is a digital divide in Egypt that runs across gender, income and geographic and social lines, with many lacking accesses to internet, computers or key technical skills. During the crisis there was the abrupt closure of school that left no time to prepare an immediate strategy and transition to online learning. In addition to that, many students have no access to technology or a suitable learning environment at home. Online learning also excludes large groups of disadvantaged students; who do not have access to online means. Other challenges include poor infrastructure and tools. Thus, the sudden shift to online schooling has raised concerns about whether Egypt's education system is equipped for such a quick scale-up of digital learning.

Introduction

Education plays an essential role in an individual's life. It is through this process that a person initially formulates his or her thoughts with the help and guidance of the instructors within the boundaries of a school. Parallel to this, it is also by means of education that individuals discover their strengths and are able to apply them to their practical life. In this regard, it is important to utilize all aspects of the learning process, including online procedures of teaching and learning that are so important in today's world. Online social networking is so important for individuals today. Understanding the contributions of online teaching for students would be a huge leap towards achieving diverse learning with minimum supervision. At the same time, the teachers would educate their students using an unconventional approach to the delivery of knowledge (Aydin, 2013).

In Egypt, there are different kinds of education, such as national curriculum, foreign curriculum, and international curriculum, offered in different kinds of instructional language, such as in Arabic and in other foreign languages, at different kinds of schools, such as in public schools, private schools, and in the international schools, etc. The quality of education, such as school facility, teaching staff, varies according to the types of schools, meeting the different needs of students, parents and stakeholder. After the sudden closure of all schools on 15 March 2020, by the Ministry of Education and Technical Education (MOETE) each type of school and its community reacted to the above MOETE-proposed measure in different ways. The COVID-19 pandemic forced schools and universities in Egypt to close and students were sent home. Learning witnessed a transformation from a traditional to a more virtual delivery method. Thus, the pandemic revealed both the opportunities and constraints of using technology for education. School closures due to (COVID-19) had been affecting students as well as teachers.

In Egypt, education is linked to the strengths of the administrator. Hence, training for teachers is regarded as very important aspect for creating and implementing a well-organized curriculum. So, the questions are: What aspect of professional training allows it to capture the attention of students? What strategies should be adopted when students are preoccupied with other activities? It is best also to highlight to the students the importance of learning without any pressure on them and to encourage participation in productive activities to heighten appreciation of their studies (Shields, 1917).

In the past, only simple tools could be used to motivate students to learn, as opposed to the variety of elements available to today's generation. Nowadays, students have varying background knowledge, readiness and languages, preferences in learning and interests, and responsive reactions. Today, societies have evolved and teachers must think creatively and engage in further exploration. However, there are also some students who make good use of the internet, and become better versed than their teachers during discussions. These are some of the reasons why teachers must be flexible in expanding their knowledge to reach the expanded horizons of the students and pull them towards the goal of becoming competitive educated people with values. Teachers must engage the students in academics to enable the students to learn and understand more. In addition, student and teacher satisfaction is an important element of quality online education especially in the COVID-19 crisis (Hall, T., Vue, G., Strangman, N., & Meyer, A., 2003). Like the rest of the world, the educational institutions in Egypt are embracing virtual and distance learning. However, the sudden shift to online schooling has raised concerns about whether Egypt's education systems are equipped for such a quick scale-up of digital learning. This is what this chapter tries to examine.

Aim of the Study

In light of the hype-surrounding internet usage and the multiple contributions of the World Wide Web in the COVID-19 crisis, there is a necessity to explore how diverse learning can emanate from internet-based teaching and learning programs. Such an exploration should also focus on investigating if teaching online can enormously be a rewarding experience for teachers as well (Poe and Stassen, n.d.) considering that the traditional system of interaction of classroom-based communication is far different from the system of online learning. Therefore, a shift to online education truly requires huge adjustments that needs to be ascertained (Karaman, 2011). This is because these shifts will likely manifest in a broader scope of services for future teachers. When shifting to an online educational environment, the alterations in learning activities require flexibility and an open-mindedness to embrace a new dimension of learning (Kim, Liu, & Bonk, 2005).

There is also a need to investigate during the COVID-19 school closure if there is an increase in the relationship between students' actual interactions and participation, as well as their learning performance. These are considerable grounds for rejecting our traditional method of teaching and learning and taking huge steps towards online education (Oliver, 1999).

Lastly, there is a need to investigate if several programs have been identified both for teachers and students as well as, consider reformatting the practice of teaching in regards to the form of online teaching and training. This training begins for prospective teachers while they are students, during their exposure to online learning.

Research Questions

This study focuses on the following research questions: Will the e-learning become a teaching strategy in Egypt overcome the challenges of the traditional lecturing style? Did Egypt have already an experience in the e-learning within the Egyptian public universities? In other words, did Egypt possess the necessary institutional higher education ICT infrastructure required for the assessment of e-learning readiness in Egypt? What is the benefit or value of students learning online? Will the adoption of the online strategy relieve student's tension and allow them to focus more on the subject matter? In particular, it is hoped this study will help provide a better understanding on the issues related to teaching and learning, in online learning both for educators, future teachers, and students. Also, the research question comes up is the undergraduate student's feedback the same as the post graduates' students?

Online Teaching and Learning Initiatives

This section describes the prospects for using the e-learning technologies in the Egyptian educational institutions during COVID-19 and thereafter. With regards to the road map for using EdTech in Egyptian universities, Egypt established since 2000 the National E-Learning Center (NELC), one of the Information and Communication Technology Project (ICTP). Its purpose was and is to serve as a technical unit within the Supreme Council of Universities to promote and support the development of e-learning in Egypt. This is to be achieved by improving the development of the learning content to the highest maturity level and to achieve strong presence both locally and regionally (Ashraf et al., 2009).

In the pre COVID-19 period, Egypt already had on the national level several programs operating to exchange knowledge and experience in educational methodologies and use advanced technologies including e-learning. Moreover, there were different e-learning initiatives since 2003 between the Egyptian Universities and international higher education institutions to develop e-content in different fields. For instance, The Arab Campus E-Learning System (ACES) is a learning-management system that provides a virtual learning environment to the students of Arab Open University, and the Egyptian E-learning University (EELU) which aims to provide distance education through 24-hour online learning with a vision to be a leading university providing e-learning nationally, regionally, and internationally (The AOU/UNESCO Collaboration, 2009).

After examining the initiatives and mechanisms put in place in Egypt to ensure that teaching and learning continue unperturbed without physical presence, it is important to briefly explore the teacher's and student's perspective from an interactive involvement. In an experience with my MBA students, they reiterated to me how they see online procedures as balancing their communication and could comprise a program that would enhance the efficiency of not only them but also the professionals and post-graduates. They were more satisfied with the interaction process. Some of them are future educators, who see online learning as a new form of shaping lives through its practicality. The post graduates' students tend to see online learning as creating a flexible environment in the educational system that could build strong knowledge out of practical moves with critical thinking. I can say that most of them were able to produce better and longer solutions to case studies, when they are participating in in-class discussions.

The key Constraints for Using EdTech in Egypt

The crisis could be summarized in the following:

1. The failure of teacher educators to adequately model the use of ICT in their own teaching/lecturing, due in part to their limited technological competence and/or their lack of understanding of the potential of ICT. Also, the lack of adequate pedagogical knowledge on the part of student teachers is an issue. There is a lack of in-depth understanding on the part of both faculty members and student teachers in pedagogy for and potential of ICT use in teaching and learning (OECD, 2015). That is, ICT should be infused into the entire curriculum so that pre-service teachers have the opportunity to understand the reasons for using ICT for educational purpose and experience how ICT can support teaching and learning across different subject domains. Without such integrated approaches, the knowledge and the skills pre-service teachers gain are likely to remain isolated and unexploited.

2. The movement to out-of-school learning exacerbated the already weak education management and data collection systems.

3.School closures left no time for schools to prepare a strategy and transition to online learning. Syllabuses which are exam-oriented do not perfectly fit in the online learning platform format. Also, the curricula could not be adapted quickly to teaching online and students faced the anxiety of not knowing how their school year will progress (David et al., 2020).

4. Many students did not have access to technology or a suitable learning environment at home. In Egypt, online learning actually excludes large groups of disadvantaged students especially those who do not have access to online means: electricity, airtime, and smartphones to interact online. Some of the problems are that some students have only low-bandwidth internet available as the national and local networks become quickly

oversaturated and slow in responding. Other challenges include poor infrastructure and tools, high illiteracy rates and languages of instruction.

5. In light of the fact that going digital does not only mean to upload lessons and/or having teachers lecture in front of a camera; it is important to prepare teachers to go digital. This includes preparedness of teachers to design and facilitate online learning. In Egypt, most teachers were not adequately prepared for the sudden transition to visual and remote school education. The parents too were not ready to facilitate and monitor daily home-based learning especially with multiple children (UNESCO, 2020).

6. Students with no access to digital devices, and students with disabilities were the most disadvantaged groups for online learning programs. Also, girls in remote areas were having a disadvantaged status in homes with fewer opportunities for accessing and using the limited number of household technological devices, and less learning time due to more home care duties (UNESCO, 2020).

7. Parents were unprepared for online learning; and were struggling to perform this task. This is especially true for parents with limited education and resources.

Opportunities of EdTech in Egypt

While COVID-19 has posed challenges in delivering education to all, it has also provided opportunities for teachers and students to innovate and to take leaps into the unknown.

1. Schools and Universities have created platforms where teachers and faculty staff can share their own EdTech solutions, hosting lesson plans and supporting materials uploaded by teachers. These platforms had already helped provide the variable abilities for teachers to use EdTech. They also multiplied the efforts of other teachers who created resources in local languages for local curricula. As a result, a wide range of open educational resources were freely available to students.

2. Many schools and universities began to rethink curriculum, as well as, curriculum-related matters, such as teaching and learning materials, classroom practices and assessment. They also began to approach teaching-learning-assessment processes differently and in a systemic way; in order to

develop students' competencies with a view to strengthening their learning skills and sustaining their motivation in the e-learning environment.

3. The current crisis constituted an opportunity to enhance student's higher- thinking skills, such as questioning, creativity and problem solving. It helped to develop important social skills, for instance empathy, working together, helping one another, being pro-active, showing initiative and students gained more autonomy; while teachers lost some opportunities for direct control and supervision.

4. The Egyptian Government increased access to digital resources. The government improved on the connectivity. This was to ensure that EdTech reach a large audience and mitigate access inequities. Also, Egyptian Government has implemented the following steps to deal with the crisis:

A) The Ministry of Education and Technical Education has thus far released a website full of helpful study guides and materials for students all over the country to access. It even includes gamified questions to make it more engaging. The Minister of Education, Tarek Shawki also that all the exams for students between third year primary school and eighth grade have been substituted with research papers for each subject. For students from Kindergarten or in first second primary grades, there won't be any examinations at all. These have been replaced with teacher's assessments based on the student's performance on the curriculum which is available on the e-library. Those in grade 10 and 11 are the only ones that have examinations. However, the way to administer the examinations has changed. They now use tablets for doing the examination via internet. Luckily, the system had already integrated technology as part of their teaching methods meaning that it will not be completely new to the students.

B) Collaborating with mobile operators, telecom providers, and other providers to increase access to digital resources.

C) Extending the access to the Egyptian Knowledge Bank (EKB) to students. That is by providing content by grade level and subject (kindergarten through secondary education). Content was available in both Arabic and English to all students, parents and teachers (does not have username/password). This site has multimedia infrastructure (videos, images, documentary films) to help explain the various lessons, and numerous full text books, including dictionaries. The EKB could be accessed by mobile phone or computer.

D) Providing a digital platform to offer a communication channel between students and teachers. This enabled approximately 22 million students distributed over 55,000 schools to communicate with teachers, explaining lessons, answering student's questions, and taking examinations online. Videos explaining how to do this are being developed; and students received a code from their teachers to enter a virtual class to continue electronically.

E) The government negotiated with the online learning provider Edmodo to deliver remote instruction to the Egypt's entire K-12 student body. Also, arrangements were made between the Ministry of Communication and IT and mobile carriers to make available SIM cards at no cost to students if they have the devices.

Recommendations of the Study

This COVID-19 pandemic and disruption has also had the potential to spark creative new partnerships to build more resilient education systems for the future. Part of that solution is focusing on remote learning opportunities both to mitigate the current disruption and build more open and flexible education systems in the coming years. Without appropriate teachers and strong leadership as well as coordination at national school levels, going digital may trigger teachers, students and parent's feeling to be overloaded and confused. Students may be flooded with homework that they and their families cannot handle. Teachers and schools should be given more space in performing formative assessments, and by turning assessments into learning opportunities. Given their usual familiarity with digital means, students should be involved in constructing these new assessment modalities that should incorporate self-assessment and assessment by peers.

Online learning can be made to provide students with many benefits and alternatives to the traditional school courses which they could not have enrolled for in home schooling. The alternatives and opportunities offered by this shift are better ways to meet the needs of the new digital age students, and a medium for receiving extra help. Thus, it is also important for teachers to be engaged with online courses in order to enable participants obtain better learning outcomes, regardless of the type of environment. This could be feasible if the following criteria are initiated:

1. Rethinking curriculum, teaching-learning-assessment processes and the development of students' competencies with a view to strengthening their learning skills and sustaining their motivation should be evaluated in order to know their lapses for the sake of strategizing for the future.

2. Investigating the effects of students' engagement in online learning. Students experience with online learning appears to be an important factor in their perceptions of learning and satisfaction.

3. Exploring whether the students valued the flexibility of online learning and opportunities to communicate with teachers and peers in an online learning setting.

4. If students can learn in online settings as effectively as in face-to-face settings, the intriguing question is: is online learning for everyone? While self-motivated students are more likely to succeed in online learning settings, it is suggested that alternative learning styles need to be addressed to make online courses available to a greater audience of students especially the disadvantaged and marginalized ones. Students who had more experience in online learning were more likely to be satisfied with learning over the Internet. They were less likely to feel anxious about online learning and are pleased with their experiences.

5. Government took actions to support students to continue their education remotely. This action was to guarantee that the online learning should be flexible and accessible where it is most needed. Government had to facilitate computer-based learning environments to equip students with a wide range of opportunities at a convenient time and a location that they prefer. These environments provide numerous online resources that can help students synthesize information through the communication that can occur during their interactions across online environments (The World Bank, 2020).

6. Exploring whether the students became open to and excited about the idea of online learning was and is necessary. This is because

online learning gives them a more creative approach towards studying and needs to be monitored in order to be able to forge ahead.

Conclusion

The COVID-19 pandemic has forced schools and universities to close and send students home. Learning witnessed a transformation from a traditional to a more virtual delivery method. School closures in response to COVID-19 exacerbated an already worrisome learning crisis in Egypt. This has placed an unprecedented risk to children's education, protection and wellbeing, especially for the hardest-to-reach, and the most marginalized. The governments have attempted to provide continuity of education through online learning, mobile phones, and printed materials with varying success. Students in Egypt have also the opportunity to continue learning and interact daily with teachers through Edmodo. The new solutions have brought many challenges and much needed innovation for the sector. Equity in access to online learning has been a major concern in the country especially for underprivileged communities who have limited or no access to free internet, electricity, computers, tablets, and other devices. Egypt addressed this challenge by providing learners with free access to online platforms and providing users with extra internet free bundles to compensate for increased internet usage. Partnership with the ministry of communication has been made to facilitate access to services and increase the speed of the internet. This reality may prove to help bridge the digital divide; as it has forced the country to find immediate solutions and innovations that will impact the education industry for a long time. It is an opportunity for Egypt to rethink education. More so, it is a call for building a more resilient and inclusive education system taking into consideration the critical role of teachers, parents, and availability of learning resources.

References

Aydin, H. (2013) Interaction between Teachers and Students in Online Learning". *Journal of Environmental Protection and Ecology*. https://www.researchgate.net/publication/287262034.

Shields, T. E. (1917). *Philosophy of Education*. Washington, DC. Catholic Education Press.

Hall, T., Vue, G., Strangman, N., & Meyer, A. (2003). Differentiated instruction and implications for UDL implementation. Wakefield, MA: National Center on Accessing the General Curriculum. (Links updated 2014).

http://aem.cast.org/about/publications/2003/ncac-differentiated-instruction-udl.html

Poe M. and Stassen M.L.A., eds., (n.d.), T*eaching and Learning Online: Communication, Community, and Assessment. A Handbook for UMass Faculty* (The University of Massachusetts, 5).

Karaman, S. (2011). "Examining the Effects of Flexible Online Exams on Students' Engagement in E-learning". *Educational Research Reviews*, Vol. 6 (3). pp. 259-264.

Kim, K. J., Liu, S. Y & Bonk, C. J. (2005). Online MBA Students' Perceptions of Online Learning: Benefits, Challenges, and Suggestions. The Internet and Higher Education 8(4), 335-344. doi: 10.1016/j.iheduc.2005.09.005

OliverRon,(1999)."ExploringStrategiesforOnlineTeachingandLearning".*Distance Education*, Vol. 20 (2). doi: 240-254, DOI: 10.1080/0158791990200205.

Ashraf S. H., Ahmed H. M., Tarek E. E., and Mohammed A. S. (2009). E-Learning in the Egyptian Public Universities: Overview and Future Prospective. Conference Paper. https://www.researchgate.net/publication/259483851

The AOU/UNESCO Collaboration. March 2009, Website: http://www.arabou.org/unesco.htm 2009.

OECD. (2015). Schools for Skills: A New Learning Agenda For Egypt. www.oecd.org/edu/policyadvice.html.

David, R., Pellini, A., Jordan, K., & Philips, T. (2020). *Education During the COVID-19 Crisis Opportunities and Constraints of Using Ed Tech in Low-Income Countries*. https://zenodo.org/record/3750976#.X2IkEoso9PY

UNESCO. (2020). COVID-19 crisis and curriculum: sustaining quality outcomes in the context of remote learning. https://unesdoc.unesco.org/ark:/48223/pf0000373273

UNESCO. (2020). *Distance Learning Strategies in Response to COVID-19 School Closures*. https://unesdoc.unesco.org/ark:/48223/pf0000373305

The World Bank. (2020). Guidance Note: Remote Learning & COVID-19. http://documents1.worldbank.org/curated/en/531681585957264427/pdf/Guidance-Note-on-Remote-Learning-and-COVID-19.pdf

Appendices

Appendix-1

Fight Against Covid 19: Updates of Covid Pandemic

11 March, 2020; World Health Organization (WHO) announced COVID-19 outbreak as a *pandemic*. As on 22.10.2020 about 215 countries and territories affected by this *pandemic* and the whole world standing at crossroad. Scientists, healthcare workers, humanist organizations and Governments are trying to do their bests to combat the situation and save human life and sufferings. It's an unsurmountable task to make the whole world population educated enough to align with the scientific approach. Due to various differences across the globe along with everchanging scientific opinion and recommendations also created many confusions. Moreover, Government and corporate level rat race in power axis also has its contribution in the whole scenario.

According to WHO report, on 23.10.2020 global situation is as follows:

Total number of affected by Covid 19 = 41,332,899

Total number of death due to Covid 19 = 1,132,879

This chapter is aimed to provide scientific information for the common man to include them in *"Fight against Covid 19"*.

For better understanding of this chapter we need to have clear idea of the following widely used terminologies.

1. **Outbreak**: The sudden or violent start or increase in rate of something unwelcome, such as war, disease, etc. In the present context its disease beginning. Sometimes, experts consider a single case of a contagious disease to be an outbreak.

2. **Contagious disease**: An infectious disease (such as influenza, measles, or tuberculosis) that is transmitted by contact with an infected individual or infected bodily discharges or fluids (such as respiratory droplets), by contact with a contaminated surface or object, or by ingestion of contaminated food or water.

NOTE: The terms *contagious disease* and *communicable disease* are often used interchangeably. However, communicable diseases such as malaria or schistosomiasis that are spread by contact with disease vectors (such as mosquitoes or ticks) are not typically considered to be "contagious" diseases since they cannot be spread from direct contact with another person.

1. **Epidemic, Pandemic and Endemic**: *-demi* (Greek *demos)* means 'people of a district.'

   a) An *epidemic* is a disease which is "affecting many persons at the same time, and spreading from person to person in a locality where the disease is not permanently prevalent.

   b) *Pandemic* is an *epidemic* that has spread over a large area, that is, it's "prevalent throughout an entire country, continent, or the whole world." Presently WHO (World Health Organization) defined as "a worldwide spread of a new disease."

   c) Endemic is an adjective that means natural to, native to, confined to, or widespread within a place or population of people. Endemic most commonly used to describe a disease that is prevalent in or restricted to a particular location, region, or population. For example, malaria is said to be endemic to tropical regions.

2. **Incubation Period:** It the time gape between person getting infected and having symptoms for that infection.

3. **Social Distancing – Isolation – Quarantine:**

   a) Physical distancing means being physically apart. WHO recommends keeping at least 1-metre distance from others.

   b) Isolation means separating people who are sick with symptoms of Covid-19 and may be infectious to prevent the spread of the disease.

c) Quarantine means restricting activities or separating people who are not ill themselves but may have been exposed to COVID-19.

Origin and nature of Covid 19

The present COVID-19 pandemic is caused by a coronavirus named *SARS-CoV-2*. Coronaviruses (CoVs) are a large family of RNA viruses, several of which cause respiratory diseases in humans, from the common cold to more rare and serious diseases such as the *Severe Acute Respiratory Syndrome (SARS)* and the *Middle East respiratory syndrome (MERS)*, both of which have high mortality rates. CoVs are divided into four genera: *alpha-*, *beta-*, *gamma-* and *delta*-CoV. Alpha- or the beta-CoV currently known to cause disease in humans. Many of these CoVs can infect several animal species as well. Usually viral infection is *species specific*. CoVs have unique character to cross *species barrier*. A virus that is regularly transmitted from an animal to a human is called a *zoonotic* virus and the first such event is called a *spillover* event. The details of genetics are beyond of the scope of this chapter. We need to understand all this for better scientific approach to combat it. As it is a new virus discovered, its is called *Novel Corona Virus*. There are many debates in the scientific community, whether Covid 19 is a naturally occurring virus or Lab. made one. Currently, the zoonotic source of SARS-CoV-2 is unknown. As per record, the first human cases of COVID-19, the coronavirus disease caused by SARS-CoV-2, were first reported from Wuhan City, China, in December 2019 (thus it's also called Covid 19).

Epidemiology and clinical presentation of Covid 19

Symptomatic transmission refers to transmission of SARS-CoV-2 from persons with symptoms, also transmission possible from asymptomatic persons. Transmission mainly occurs from symptomatic people to others by :

- close contact through respiratory droplets,
- direct contact with infected persons,
- contact with contaminated objects and surfaces by body fluids.

Main root of entry to human body through nose, mouth cavity and eyes. Incubation period usually 2 to 14 days, can be up to 27 days.

Symptomatic patients may have mild to severe disease manifestation. Comorbid medical disorders have cumulative negative impact. So far death rate is approximately 3.5 %.

According to the clinical severity, it classified mainly three groups, namely mild moderate and severe.

Management of Covid 19

Understanding Health and Healthcare:

Health is a State of complete Physical, Mental and Social wellbeing, and not merely the absence of disease or infirmity (as defined by W.H.O). Healthcare is organized efforts made to maintain health or treat disease. Therefore, healthcare is the actions takes for restoration of health and disease prevention, control and cure. In the definition itself, 'health' has three main parameters, namely physical, mental and social parameters. Though we usually understand the physical parameter first, then mental parameter and lastly social parameter. Maintaining overall health is a costly affair, both for individual and at Governmental level. Healthcare industry not only maintaining health but also approaching towards super health to achieve a state called Post Human. Developed countries spend about 7 to 10 % of their GDP in healthcare. In case of India its only about 3 % of national GDP. So, the resources are not unlimited and we need to manage this Covid -19 pandemic within the available resources.

Covid-19 Management Planning:

The Covid-19 is a new virus in human history. Various trials and recommendations are in place to combat. Also, tireless attempts to make an effective vaccine for covid-19 are at war footings. The *Strategic preparedness and response plan* outline main objectives for COVID-19 are to:

- slow and stop transmission;
- provide optimized care for all patients; and
- minimize the impact of the epidemic on health systems, social services and economic activity.

The management protocol is depending upon policy of the government, locally available resources and their optimized coordinated utilization. In every stage of care the basic principles of precautionary measures (hand hygiene, PPE, face musk, face cover etc.) are maintained all the time. However, the fundamental pathway is similar in all the regions as outlined below;

Step I: Screen for Civid-19: Screening and questioner-based suspicion and followed by RT-PCR (*Reverse Transcriptase – Polymerase Chain Reaction*) for Covid-19 is the mainstay of detecting positive cases. Protection of healthcare workers and caregivers are utmost important. In any pandemic condition screening is the essential tool for management. Swab from nasopharynx and/or oropharynx is technically easy to implement for mass screening activity.

Step II: Acuity-based triage: In emergency care set up, patients need to categorize and provide time sensitive emergency care.

Step III: Clinical Assessment: Before starting any medical treatment assessment for severity of the disease, including risk factors and other existing disease need to evaluate thoroughly.

Step IV: Treatment for Covid-19: At preset time, neither anti-Covid-19 medicine nor vaccine nor any effective prophylaxis available for treatment of covid-19 diseases. Supportive care and management of existing diseases as per protocol is the treatment. In this context many treatment protocols are in trial. Till date no specific medication recommended by reputed authorities like WHO, CDC etc. Details of treatment modalities are beyond the scope of this chapter.

Step V: Post recovery care: Once a patient recovers from covid-19 disease he needs special care to come back to his normal life and prevention from reinfection. Post recovery care depends heavily depends on community care facilities.

Vaccine for Covid 19

Vaccines greatly reduce the risk of infection by training the immune system to recognize and fight pathogens. There are many successful vaccines to prevent viral diseases, such as measles, polio, hepatitis B, influenza and many others. When most people in a community are vaccinated for a disease, the ability of the pathogen to spread is limited. This is called 'herd' or 'indirect' or 'population' immunity. Nevertheless, when many people have immunity, that also indirectly protects people who cannot be vaccinated, such as very young babies and those who have compromised immune systems. Vaccines are designed to deliver an immunogen which is a specific type of antigen that elicits an immune response, so that the immune system able recognize the pathogen when it is encountered naturally. Usual root of vaccine administration in intramuscular, subcuticular, nasal or oral. Vaccine may be of single dosed or sequenced multiple doses. There are many projects around the world going on to develop an effective vaccine for Covid-19, but still none is available as of today. We hope to get effective one within a short period of time.

Synopsis of various relevant points

Amongst so many scientific and technical details its difficult for a common man to give an effort towards sustainability of health in this pandemic. As a civilized society we can definitely contribute for each other by maintaining social norms aligned with scientific guidelines. Whatever is the stage, few basic things are constant and clear understanding is must.

a) **Social distancing:** To prevent transmission from one person to another person, personal distancing in one of the most important factors. WHO recommends 1 meter personal / physical distance for Covid-19. CDC added time of exposure in this criterion. As per CDC recommendation it should be less than total 20 minutes exposure in 24 hours. Together with social distancing and protective personal equipment evidence showed a significant reduction of spread of Covid-19.

b) **Hand washing / sanitizing:** Frequent hand washing with soap and water is recommended to prevent Covid-19. The rubbing of hands to be at least 30 seconds. Whenever hand washing with soap and water not possible, alcohol-based hand sanitizer (80% alcohol) may be used. Hand washing is extremely important as we tend to touch and rub our eyes, nose and mouth by hands. There are many surface disinfectants also easily available in the market.

c) **PPE (personal protective equipment):** These are external protective wearables which prevent transmission. Amongst many things Face musk, Face shield, gloves and body suite are particularly important.

- **Non-medical, fabric masks** are advised for use by the general public when physical distancing cannot be maintained, as part of a comprehensive '**Do it all!**' approach, including improving ventilation; cleaning hands; covering sneezes and coughs, and more. This type of musk can be washed and reused.
- **Medical masks are** recommended for the following groups:
  - ➢ All health workers in clinical settings.
  - ➢ Anyone who is feeling unwell, including people with mild symptoms, such as muscle aches, slight cough, sore throat or fatigue.
  - ➢ People caring for suspected or confirmed cases of COVID-19 outside of health facilities.
- When one can't guarantee a distance of at least 1 metre from others, medical masks are also recommended for the following groups, as they are at a higher risk of becoming seriously ill with COVID-19 and dying:
  - ➢ People aged 60 or over.
  - ➢ People of any age with underlying health conditions, including: chronic respiratory disease, cardiovascular disease, cancer, obesity, immunocompromised patients and diabetes mellitus.
- Medical masks (also known as surgical masks)
- Made of three layers of synthetic nonwoven materials Configured to have filtration layers sandwiched in the middle. Available in different thicknesses. Have various levels of fluid-resistance and filtration. Respirators (also known as filtering facepiece respirators - FFP) are available at different performance levels such as FFP2, FFP3, N95, N99 and designed to protect healthcare workers who provide care to COVID-19 patients in settings and areas where aerosol generating procedures are undertaken.
- Face shield and gloves are not for use by common man, who is not directly involved in covid-19 care.

- Body suites are for healthcare providers dealing with covid-19 patients.
- Children aged 5 years and under do not be required to wear masks, unless specifically indicated. This is based on the safety and overall interest of the child and the capacity to appropriately use a mask with minimal assistance.

Based on the above-mentioned basic facts, our life style needs to change in collective way to fight against Covid-19. We will discuss few important aspects of implementation during this pandemic.

1. **New born and children:** They can be infected and cause transmission like adults. Though rate of getting serious disease manifestation is very low. Usual care with basic hygiene is sufficient to deal with. All vaccinations to be given as per schedule. Special care for psychological health of children is recommended as there are restrictions on free movements in public spaces and mixing up with peer groups. Encourage children for physical activity and creative works. Need to be vigilant about child abuse.
2. **Young adults:** This group usually don't affect with serious covid-19 disease. They have special psycho-somatic requirements. They are more stressed with boyfriends / girlfriends and career. Daily physical activity, creative work and care for sexual health are important.
3. **Pregnancy and breast feeding:** Covid-19 is not any contraindication to getting pregnant. Usual pregnancy care with protection for covid-19 needed. There are evidences suggestive of transplacental crossover of covid-19, from positive mother to the fetus, but no evidence of severe disease of the new born baby. There is no correlation of delivery method (normal or caesarian) and covid-19 status of the pregnant woman; that has to be decided by the patient and treating doctor as per usual norms.

There are no data suggestive of transmission of active COVID-19 (virus that can cause infection) through breast milk and breastfeeding has not been detected to date. There is no reason to avoid or stop breastfeeding. In all socio-economic settings, breastfeeding recommended as it improves survival and provides lifelong health and development advantages to newborns and infants as well as mother. Breastfeeding recommended even by confirmed Covid-19 positive mother with some preauction, eg.

i) Washing hands frequently with soap and water or use alcohol-based hand rub and especially before touching the baby;

ii) Wear a medical grade mask during any contact with the baby, including while feeding;

iii) Sneeze or cough into a tissue. Then dispose of it immediately and wash hands again;

iv) Routinely clean and disinfect surfaces that mothers have touched.

v) If mother is very sick then expressed or donor breast milk recommended.

1. **Sexual health:** There is no evidence that COVID-19 is transmitted through semen or vaginal fluids. However, having sex with someone means that they are very close to each other. This puts one person at risk if the other person has COVID-19. Masturbation does not involve another person, and carries no risk of COVID-19. Also, having sex itself not a risk of covid-19. Need to be vigilant about sexual harassment, women in particular.

2. **Senior citizen at home:** Senior citizen are more vulnerable due to age and other comorbidities eg, Diabetes, hypertension, renal failure, cancer etc. Usual protection for covid-19 along with continuation of all regular medication for other diseases are the recommendation. Keeping handy the emergency contacts and access to medicines, essentials, food supply and health care are utmost important. Special attention about mental health required. Grand children and pets are good time pass for them. Pets can be infected from human (who is infected) but other way round is not documented.

3. **Grocery and food items:** There's no evidence of anyone infected with COVID-19 after touching food containers and food packaging, though virus can survive variable time in various surfaces. Maintaining hand hygiene and washing vegetables with running water is acceptable. Drinking water, food items, playground, swimming pool are safe so far covid-19 is concerned.

4. **Surface cleaning at home:** Disinfection practices are important to reduce the transmission of COVID-19, such as in the home, office, schools, gyms, publicly accessible buildings, religious centers, markets, transportation and business settings or restaurants. High-touch surfaces are in priority for disinfection such as door and window handles, kitchen and food preparation areas, counter tops, bathroom surfaces, toilets and taps, touchscreen personal devices, personal computer keyboards, and work surfaces. Sodium hypochlorite solution (0.1%) or Alcohol (70-90%) can also be used for surface disinfection.

5. **Travelling:** It's better to be avoided if not essential one. Regulation varies from country to country. So far technology is concern keeping other factors at same place, air travel is safest mode of transport in comparison with other mode of public transport. ICAO, IATA, WHO has many international announcements / recommendations regarding safety measures for air transport in covid-19 pandemic to minimize transmission of disease.

6. **Public gathering:** All types of public gatherings, small or big; are to be avoided. In unavoidable circumstances open space, hand washing, social distancing, musk, surface cleaning with recommended disinfectant etc. must be taken care off. Government and local authorities are providing many guidelines which are to keep in mind in that circumstances.

7. **Accommodation facilities:** Hostels, hotels etc. are place where accommodation can't be avoided as these are essential part of modern life. Ventilation is an important factor in preventing COVID-19 from spreading. Recirculated air from split air conditioning units, fan coils or any system that runs with a recirculation mode should be avoided where possible, unless in a single occupancy room with none else present. If recirculation is unavoidable, increase outdoor air exchange by opening windows, if possible and safe to do so, and minimize air blowing from one person directly at another. Floor or ceiling fans can provide ventilation when the people occupying the room are from the same household, but are not recommended when travellers from different households are together.

Take home points

1. Hand wash / sanitizer, social distancing and musk use are essential part to manage covid-19 pandemic.
2. Most of us will survive in covid pandemic.
3. Presently there is no specific (antiviral) medicine for protection / cure from covid-19 recommended or available.
4. Till date no vaccine is available for covid-19.
5. No food item, vegetable, vitamins, minerals, food supplements can cure covid-19.
6. Alcohol, smoking, drugs etc. do not protect from covid-19, can be dangerous.
7. Sunray, cold atmosphere, hot bath etc. not protection from covid-19.
8. Mosquito bite, house flies, pets do not transmit covid-19 to human.
9. People of all ages can be infected.
10. Thermal scanner doesn't detect covid-19.

References

WHO/2019-nCoV/FAQ/Virus_origin/2020.1

WHO/2019-nCoV/clinical/2020.5

WHO/2019-nCoV/IPC_Masks/Children/2020.1

Appendix -2

CDC expands definition of who is a 'close contact' of an individual with Covid-19

Federal health officials issued new guidance on 22 October 2020, that greatly expands the pool of people considered at risk of contracting the novel coronavirus by changing the definition of who is a "close contact" of an infected individual.

The change by the Centers for Disease Control and Prevention is likely to have its biggest impact in schools, workplaces and other group settings where people are in contact with others for long periods of time. It also underscores the importance of mask-wearing to prevent spread of the virus, even as President Trump and his top coronavirus adviser continue to raise doubts about such guidance.

The CDC had previously defined a "close contact" as someone who spent at least 15 consecutive minutes within six feet of a confirmed coronavirus case. The updated guidance, which health departments rely on to conduct contact tracing, now defines a close contact as someone who was within six feet of an infected individual for a total of 15 minutes or more over a 24-hour period, according to a CDC statement on 22 October 2020.

Superspreader events are the leading cause of coronavirus transmission in the U.S. Here's what they entail, and why they are so dangerous. (Adriana Usero/The Washington Post)

The update comes as the United States is "unfortunately seeing a distressing trend, with cases increasing in nearly 75 percent of the country," Jay Butler, the CDC's deputy director for infectious diseases, said Wednesday at CDC headquarters in Atlanta, in the first news conference administration officials permitted in more than eight weeks. People may be tired of the advice, Butler said, but mask-wearing is more important than ever this fall and winter as Americans head indoors, where transmission risks are greater.

The guidance about transmission of the coronavirus, which causes covid-19, had been discussed by CDC scientists for several weeks, according to a CDC official who spoke on the condition of anonymity to share policy discussions. Then came unsettling new evidence in a report published Wednesday. CDC and Vermont health officials discovered the virus was contracted by a 20-year-old prison employee who in an eight-hour shift had 22 interactions — for a total of over 17 minutes — with individuals who later tested positive for the virus.

"Available data suggests that at least one of the asymptomatic [infectious detainees] transmitted" the virus during these brief encounters, the report said.

"This article adds to the scientific knowledge of the risk to contacts of those with covid-19 and highlights again the importance of wearing face masks to prevent transmission," the CDC said.

As many as half of all people who have the virus don't show symptoms, "so it's critical to wear a mask because you could be carrying the virus and not know it," the CDC said. "While a mask provides some limited protection to the wearer, each additional person who wears a mask increases the individual protection for everyone. When more people wear masks, more people are protected."

Caitlin Rivers, an epidemiologist at the Johns Hopkins Center for Health Security, called the updated guidance an important change.

"It's easy to accumulate 15 minutes in small increments when you spend all day together — a few minutes at the water cooler, a few minutes in the elevator, and so on," Rivers said. "I expect this will result in many more people being identified as close contacts."

She added: "This change underscores the importance of vigilant social distancing — even multiple brief interactions can pose a risk."

At the same time, Rivers said, it's not clear whether the multiple brief encounters were the only explanation for how the prison employee became infected. Other potential pathways might have been airborne or surface transmission of the virus. She also noted that the new guidance "will be difficult for contact tracing programs to implement, and schools and businesses will have a difficult time operating under this guidance."

Tom Frieden, who was CDC director during the Obama administration, called the guidance "a sensible change." But he also said that "whether someone is a contact depends on the exposure, environment and infectivity of the source patient."

Both presidential campaigns have relied on the CDC's previous definitions of "close contact" to determine when candidates and staff members need to be quarantined. A spokesman for Vice President Pence, who was in a room with Trump two days before his positive diagnosis, said the vice president did not meet the new definition of "close contact" either.

In the last week, both Democratic presidential nominee Joe Biden and Sen. Kamala D. Harris have been near charter airline workers who have tested positive for the virus. Harris also had a staff member test positive. Biden campaign manager Jen O'Malley Dillon said previously that none of those interactions qualified as "close contacts" under the old guidelines.

At the Vermont prison, the correctional worker had multiple brief encounters on 28 July with six prisoners while their coronavirus test results were pending. The next day, all six individuals tested positive. The Vermont health and correction authorities conducted a contact tracing investigation and determined the officer did not meet the definition of a close contact, and he continued to work.

But a week later, the employee had symptoms of covid-19, including loss of smell and taste, runny nose, cough, shortness of breath, and loss of appetite. He got tested the next day and on 11 August found out he was positive.

Vermont authorities reviewed 28 July video surveillance footage and determined the employee never spent 15 consecutive minutes within six feet of any of the infected individuals. But the employee did have "numerous brief (approximately one-minute) encounters that cumulatively exceeded 15 minutes." During his eight-hour shift, he was within six feet of an infected person an estimated 22 times, for a total of about 17 minutes of exposure, according to the CDC report.

The officer wore a cloth mask, gown and eye protection during all of the interactions. The infected individuals wore masks during most interactions with him. However, they were not masked during several that took place in a cell doorway and a prison recreation room, the report said.

The officer reported no other known close contact exposures to individuals with the coronavirus outside work, and did not travel outside Vermont during the 14 days before he got sick, the report said. Investigators said "his most likely exposures occurred in the correctional facility" through the multiple brief encounters.

Michael Scherer contributed to this report.

Reference:

https://www.washingtonpost.com/health/2020/10/21/coronavirus-close-contact-cdc/

Appendix-3

TYPES OF COVID-19 VACCINES

This primer outlines key terms and concepts related to Covid-19 vaccines and is intended for members of the general public, policy makers, educators, and key stakeholders.

International Vaccine Access Center

This primer on Covid-19 vaccines consists of a series of brief reports on vaccine development, allocation, and deployment in the United States and globally. The intended audience is the general public as well as policymakers, educators, and key stakeholders interested in a concise guide to Covid-19 vaccines. Topics to be addressed include ensuring the safety and efficacy of Covid-19 vaccines, principles for vaccine allocation, strategies for deployment and delivery of Covid-19 vaccines, vaccine confidence and demand, and the economics of Covid-19 vaccines.

Types of COVID-19 Vaccines

Several different types of vaccines against SARS-CoV-2, the virus that causes the disease Covid-19, are in development. Some are based on traditional methods for producing vaccines and others use newer methods.

Vaccines stimulate the human body's own protective immune responses so that, if a person is infected with a pathogen, the immune system can quickly prevent the infection from spreading within the body and causing disease. In this way, vaccines mimic natural infection but without actually causing a person to become sick.

For SARS-CoV-2, antibodies that bind to and block the spike protein on the virus's surface are thought to be most important for protection from disease because the spike protein is what attaches to human cells, allowing the virus to enter. Blocking this entrance prevents infection and thus disease and transmission to others.

Desired Vaccine Characteristics

The ideal SARS-CoV-2 vaccine would:

1. be safe and associated with only mild, transient side effects (e.g. soreness and low-grade fever);
2. confer long-lasting protection (more than a season) in a high proportion of vaccine recipients (e.g. >80%), particularly in vulnerable populations such as the older adults and those with other underlying medical conditions or risk factors such as obesity;
3. protect not only against disease but prevent virus transmission to others;
4. be administered as a single dose;
5. be able to be produced quickly and in large quantities;
6. be easily stored (e.g., not at ultra-low temperatures, in packaging that does not require a lot of space);
7. can be easily transported (e.g., outside of the cold-chain or even through the mail); and
8. can be easily administered (does not require special devices, self-administered or administered by those who do not require much training).

The initial SARS-CoV-2 vaccines will not have all of these characteristics and we may never have a vaccine that does. Different types of vaccines will have different characteristics with different tradeoffs. The most important characteristics are that a SARS-CoV-2 vaccine be safe, shortly after vaccination and in the long term, and protect a substantial proportion of those vaccinated against moderate to severe disease, particularly those in the most vulnerable groups.

Inactivated Virus Vaccines

Several inactivated SARS-CoV-2 vaccines have been developed, including those by Sinovac Biotech, Sinopharm, the Wuhan Institute of Biological Products, and Bharat Biotech. Inactivation of viruses is a well-established method to produce vaccines and several inactivated virus vaccines are widely used, including vaccines against influenza, polio, hepatitis A, and rabies viruses. The virus is inactivated so that it can no longer replicate or multiply. The immune system is exposed to viral proteins but the inactivated virus cannot cause disease. The inactivated virus stimulates the body's immune system to produce antibodies so when a person is exposed to the natural virus, antibodies are called to action to fight the virus.

Production of inactivated virus vaccines requires the ability to cultivate or grow the virus in large quantities. Because viruses cannot replicate outside of host cells, vaccine viruses need to be cultured in continuous cell lines or tissues. Influenza virus, for example, is typically grown in eggs to produce the inactivated influenza vaccine. The virus is then purified and concentrated before inactivation with chemicals. Inactivated vaccines typically do not provide immune responses as strong as attenuated (i.e., modified or weakened viruses so they do not cause disease) viral vaccines and may require booster doses to achieve and sustain protection.

Inactivated virus vaccines have been produced for many decades and the manufacturing procedures are well established and relatively straightforward, although there are challenges to producing safe and effective inactivated virus vaccines. First, the inactivation process has to sufficiently inactivate all of the virus without changing viral proteins so much that they induce weak immune responses. Second, the inactivation process cannot alter the virial proteins in a way that results in an abnormal or altered immune response and enhanced disease after exposure to the natural virus. As with all vaccines, the immunogenicity of new inactivated virus vaccines must be rigorously tested to ensure safety and efficacy.

Protein-Based Vaccines

Many vaccines for SARS-CoV-2 in development include only viral proteins and no genetic material, including those by Novavax, Sanofi and GlaxoSmithKline, SpyBiotech, and others. Some use whole viral proteins and others just pieces of viral proteins. For SARS-CoV-2 vaccines, this means either the spike protein on the surface of the virus or a portion of the spike protein called the receptor-binding domain, which binds to host cells (i.e., the cells where viruses can replicate). These protein-based, or subunit, vaccines work much like inactivated vaccines by exposing the immune system to viral proteins and inducing protective immune responses without causing disease. In the case of protein-based vaccines, this is because no genes necessary for virus replication are included in the vaccine.

Protein-based vaccines have been widely used and have a long history of safety and effectiveness. Examples include vaccines for hepatitis B virus, shingles, and the bacteria that cause whooping cough (pertussis). There are different ways of producing recombinant viral proteins, including production of the virus protein in yeast or insect cells. Protein-based vaccines also can be packaged in different ways and combined with vaccine adjuvants (additives in small quantities) that improve or enhance immune responses. The Novavax SARS-CoV-2 vaccine, for example, uses nanoparticles of cholesterol, phospholipid, and saponins from the soap bark tree to deliver viral proteins to cells of the immune system and stimulate strong immune responses.

The addition of adjuvants to vaccines is another common way of enhancing the immune responses to virus proteins. Protein-based vaccines sometimes do not induce strong CD8 T cell responses, the cells that destroy virus-infected cells, and adjuvants can help correct this. Aluminum-containing adjuvants have been used in vaccines since the 1930s in small enough quantities to not cause any harm. Other adjuvants include different lipid formulations and a synthetic form of DNA that mimics bacterial and viral genetic material. Vaccine adjuvants will likely be important to induce strong and durable protection in older adults whose immune systems are less responsive as they age. Vaccines with adjuvants can cause more local reactions, such as redness, swelling, and pain at the injection site, and more systemic reactions such as fever, chills, and body aches, than non-adjuvanted vaccines.

Viral Vector Vaccines

Viral vector vaccines use another non-replicating virus to deliver SARS-CoV-2 genes, in the form of DNA, into human cells where viral proteins are produced to induce protective immune responses. This viral DNA is not integrated into the host genome (i.e.., all of the body's DNA) but is transcribed or copied into messenger RNA and translated into proteins. Current SARS-CoV-2 viral vectored vaccines use non-replicating human or chimpanzee adenoviruses, including those by AstraZeneca with the University of Oxford, Johnson & Johnson, CanSino Biologics, and the Gamaleya Research Institute, part of Russia's Ministry of Health.

Adenoviruses are a group of approximately 50 common viruses that can cause cold-like symptoms, fever, sore throat, diarrhea, and pink eye. The human adenovirus vectors used for SARS-CoV-2 are weakened forms of adenovirus 5 and adenovirus 26. The weakened vectors do not replicate because important genes have been deleted. These vaccines will likely require at least two doses, although there is some hope that a single dose may induce protective immune responses.

Viral vectors have been studied for several decades for gene therapy, to treat cancer, and for research into molecular biology as well as for vaccines. Viral vectors other than adenoviruses include retroviruses and the vaccinia virus that was used to prevent smallpox. In July 2020, the European Commission approved use of an adenovirus 26 vaccine for Ebola that was manufactured by Johnson & Johnson, the first adenovirus vectored vaccine approved for use in humans, and the same vaccine platform used by Johnson & Johnson for their SARS-CoV-2 vaccine. Large-scale production of viral vector vaccines requires cultivation of the viral vector, such as adenovirus, in cell cultures and virus purification.

Most people have been exposed to multiple adenoviruses and thus have pre-existing immunity that could impair vector entry into host cells. This is a potential limitation of viral vector vaccines using human adenoviruses. The AstraZeneca and University of Oxford vaccine uses a chimpanzee adenovirus as vector, thus minimizing the risk of pre-existing immunity to the vector that might reduce vaccine efficacy.

Genetic Vaccines

Instead of using a viral vector to deliver SARS-CoV-2 virus genes to human cells, the genes can be administered directly as either DNA or RNA. Several of the SARS-CoV-2 vaccines furthest along in phase 3 trials are messenger RNA (mRNA) vaccines that deliver the spike protein gene, including those by Moderna, BioNTec with Pfizer, CureVac, Inovio, and Imperial College London. Once the genetic sequence of the SARS-CoV-2 virus was known in January 2020, it was relatively straightforward to generate genetic vaccine candidates.

RNA vaccines are easier to develop and manufacture compared to other vaccine types as they do not require cultivating viruses in cells. This is why they were some of the first SARS-CoV-2 vaccines to enter human trials. However, no mRNA vaccine has previously been licensed and approved for humans and most experience with this technology in humans has been for the treatment of cancer.

RNA vaccines are taken up into cells, but do not need to enter the nucleus to trick the body into producing viral proteins, which then induce immune responses. RNA is particularly potent at inducing innate immune response, the earliest type of response to a pathogen that prevents spread within the body. mRNA is used by the cell as a template to build a protein through the process of translation.

Early phase 1 and 2 studies of SARS-CoV-2 RNA vaccines show these vaccines induce immune responses likely to be protective, including in older adults. However, until phase 3 clinical trials are completed, the safety, efficacy, and duration of protection from mRNA vaccines will not be known and at least two doses will be required.

Advantages And Disadvantages of Different Vaccine Types

Until completion of the phase 3 clinical trials, we will not know the safety and efficacy of the different types of SARS-CoV-2 vaccines and their relative advantages and disadvantages. It will be important to not only monitor short-term vaccine safety, such as soreness and fever, but the risk of long-term adverse events such as enhanced disease following exposure to natural infection and autoimmune diseases. Of particular interest will be vaccine effectiveness in vulnerable populations such as older adults and those with underlying medical conditions, including diabetes, HIV infection, and chronic heart, kidney, and lung diseases. Protein-based vaccines with adjuvants may be the most likely to induce protective immune responses in elderly adults with weakened immune systems. These different vaccine types will not be interchangeable. Once a vaccine is selected, the same vaccine must be used for a second dose if required.

Many of the vaccines furthest along in development are those for which vaccine delivery platforms existed. mRNA vaccines were developed rapidly after the SARS-CoV-2 genome was sequenced and manufacturing capacity can be rapidly scaled-up. However, some mRNA vaccines have stringent cold chain requirements. The Pfizer and BioNTech mRNA will need to be stored at -70oC until about 48 hours prior to use, when it can be refrigerated, because of the instability of RNA, while the Moderna mRNA vaccine may require storage at -20oC until about one week prior to use. Freezers with the capacity to hold large volumes of vaccine at this temperature will be needed and are not currently part of the existing vaccine supply cold chain.

Source: https://coronavirus.jhu.edu/vaccines/reports/types-of-covid-19-vaccines

Appendix- 4

Global Covid-19 cases top 43.3mn: Johns Hopkins

As of 27 October 2020 morning, the total number of cases stood at 43,438,043, while the death toll surged to 1,158,882, the University's Center for Systems Science and Engineering (CSSE) revealed in its latest update.

The US is the worst-hit country with the world's highest number of cases and deaths at 8,700,053 and 225,696, respectively, according to the CSSE.

India comes in second place in terms of cases at 7,909,959, while the country's death toll soared to 119,014.

The other top 15 countries with the maximum amount of cases are Brazil (5,409,854), Russia (1,520,800), France (1,209,651), Argentina (1,102,301), Spain (1,098,320), Colombia (1,025,052), the UK (897,740), Mexico (895,326), Peru (888,715), South Africa (716,759), Iran (574,856), Italy (542,789), Chile (503,598), Iraq (455,398) and Germany (450,258), the CSSE figures showed.

Brazil currently accounts for the second highest number of fatalities at 157,397.

The countries with a death toll above 10,000 are Mexico (89,171), the UK (45,088), Italy (45,088), France (35,052), Spain (35,031), Peru (34,149), Iran (32,953), Colombia (30,348), Argentina (29,301), Russia (26,092), South Africa (19,008), Chile (14,003), Indonesia (13,411), Ecuador (12,573), Belgium (10,810), Iraq (10,671), Germany (10,074) and Canada (10,026).

Source: https://www.weeklyvoice.com/global-covid-19-cases-top-43-3mn -johns- hopkins/

Appendix-5

USAID: COVID-19 GLOBAL RESPONSE - FACT SHEET #9 FY20

9 September, 2020

Key Developments

Since the emergence of the coronavirus disease (COVID-19) in early 2020, the United States Agency for International Development (USAID) has worked in partnership with the U.S. Department of State (DoS), the National Security Council (NSC), and other parts of the interagency to lead the U.S. Government's global response, track the spread of the outbreak, and direct assistance to affected countries. Since its establishment on 9 March, USAID's COVID-19 Task Force has led the Agency's efforts to protect the safety and security of USAID's global workforce, ensure the Agency could continue its life-saving mission across the world, and support partner countries in their response to COVID-19. On 9 September, the COVID-19 Task Force finalized the transition of core responsibilities back to various parts of the Agency, ensuring that all essential operational and logistical functions enable USAID to continue its important work of responding to the COVID-19 pandemic.

To date, pledged funding from USAID includes $299 million in assistance from USAID's Emergency Reserve Fund for Contagious Infectious-Disease Outbreaks (ERF-USAID), $235 million in Global Health Programs (GHP-USAID) funds, $558 million in humanitarian assistance from USAID's International Disaster Assistance (IDA) account, and $243 million from the Economic Support Fund (ESF). USAID's Bureau for Humanitarian Assistance (USAID/BHA) leveraged the $558 million in IDA to support the COVID-19 response through 220 awards across 41 countries.

In coordination with the NSC, USAID is working with U.S. Government (USG) interagency partners, including the U.S. Department of Defense, and the private sector to fulfill U.S. President Donald J. Trump's commitment to provide ventilators to countries in need. To date, USAID has announced delivery of more than 6,100 ventilators to Bolivia, Brazil, Colombia, Dominican Republic, Ecuador, Egypt, El Salvador, Ethiopia, Fiji, Haiti, Honduras, India, Indonesia, Kiribati, Kosovo, Mozambique, Nauru, Nigeria, Pakistan, Panama, Papua New Guinea, Paraguay, Peru, the Philippines, Russia, Rwanda, South Africa, Sri Lanka, Saint Kitts and Nevis, and Uzbekistan to support care for COVID-19 patients.

USAID will also continue to support democracy, human rights, and governance programming by advancing press and civic freedom by monitoring legal protections for journalists and civil society organizations (CSOs); providing legal assistance where governments have used COVID-19-related emergency laws to restrict rights; promote media integrity and communicate information on COVID-19; counter misinformation and disinformation; and support CSOs to promote transparent governance.

Global

USAID's Bureau for Resilience and Food Security (USAID/RFS) received $8 million in ESF COVID-19 funding, which USAID/RFS is utilizing to support efforts to mitigate impacts on food and water security, livelihoods, and nutrition related to COVID-19. USAID/RFS partners are working to combat these second order impacts of the pandemic through facilitating data-driven policy development and analysis; fostering the dissemination of context-specific information to strengthen safe food distribution systems and functioning markets; and supporting critical small- and medium-sized agri-food enterprises through access to finance and technical support services to help adapt business models while strengthening production systems. USAID/RFS is also using the Scientific Animations Without Borders (SAWBO) tool to rapidly disseminate key messages on mitigating COVID-19 impacts using science-based animations. These messages are distributed in local languages via virtual platforms to reach remote and marginalized communities and demonstrate simple ways for farmers and businesses to plant, store harvested crops, and conduct market transactions while preventing the spread of COVID-19

AFRICA

USAID partner JHPIEGO is providing technical assistance and critical care support for COVID-19 case management at two treatment centers in Lesotho. As of 10 August, the project had supported a total of more than 160 patient admissions at the two centers. In addition, the non-governmental organization (NGO) provided training to nearly 900 clinical staff and more than 800 non-clinical staff on national COVID-19 clinical guidelines across 14 hospitals. These critical care interventions are crucial in bolstering health care providers' capacity to identify, manage, and treat individuals diagnosed with COVID-19 throughout the country.

With USAID support in Mali, partner Johns Hopkins University (JHU) worked with national agencies to promote and regularly update "STOPCOVID19"—the Ministry of Health's web page dedicated to COVID-19—and amplify the Ministry's call center as a source for reliable information. Through these and other efforts, JHU reached an estimated 8.8 million people via television, radio, social media, and print media in the country.

In Cameroon, USAID partner the UN Children's Fund (UNICEF) supported 115 community radio stations to broadcast spots on COVID-19 prevention and deliver interactive programs to collect and address feedback from communities. Through these radio programs, approximately 600,000 people received messaging regarding the risks of and prevention techniques for COVID-19.

With $2 million in USAID assistance, the Agency for Technical Cooperation and Development (ACTED) is supporting humanitarian health, protection, and water, sanitation, and hygiene (WASH) activities in five prefectures in the Central African Republic (CAR). To prevent the spread of COVID-19 among communities in the prefectures, the NGO is conducting risk communication and community engagement (RCCE) activities to message health risks related to the disease, as well as promoting hygiene practices for COVID-19 prevention at the household level. In addition, ACTED is installing handwashing stations in communal areas and distributing hygiene kits and other supplies to vulnerable households in CAR.

To support communities in Mozambique in understanding and mitigating the risks of COVID-19, CARE is providing hygiene promotion and health messaging support with $1 million in USAID support. The NGO is printing and distributing materials to inform households of risks related to the disease, as well as conducting health education sessions and communicating health and hygiene information approved by the Government of Mozambique Ministry of Health, in three provinces in the country. Additionally, to ensure communities can practice safe hygiene to limit the spread of COVID-19, CARE is working to repair non-functioning water points, distributing treated water and providing water trucking services, and distributing other WASH supplies.

ASIA

In Bangladesh, JHU reached an estimated 20.6 million individuals via radio and an estimated 56.9 million individuals via televised public service announcements in July to address myths and disseminate accurate information about COVID-19. In addition, JHU engaged nearly 116,200 health care providers in an online course to provide technical support to address the mental and physical challenges of the COVID-19 response, including proper use of personal protective equipment (PPE), self-care techniques, and protection of family members.

USAID partner Chemonics supported laboratory skills training for 85 staff from 24 laboratories in 19 provinces of Indonesia. Facilitated by 10 national officials and experts from other organizations, the training is helping build capacity to respond to the COVID-19 outbreak in the country.

In Pakistan, USAID partner John Snow International (JSI) has trained nearly 2,900 health staff to serve on District Rapid Response teams throughout the country. The function of these teams includes active case finding, contact tracing, monitoring and reporting, sample collection, storage and transportation, infection prevention and control, risk communication, community engagement, and safe burial practices.

With $2.8 million in USAID support, Acción contra el Hambre (ACH) is working to reduce the spread of COVID-19 among communities affected by conflict and earthquakes in the Philippines through emergency health and WASH programs. ACH is providing training for health care staff and volunteers, conducting public messaging to raise awareness of COVID-19, and working to improve vulnerable populations' access to handwashing facilities. In addition, the NGO is incorporating COVID-19 risk awareness messaging into its WASH programming, which supports approximately 13,500 people in the country's Lanao del Sur Province. ACH's messaging emphasizes the importance of handwashing, adhering to physical distancing guidelines, and wearing a mask during distributions of assistance.

To support the health system and help communities in hard-to-reach areas respond to the COVID-19 outbreak, a USAID partner is conducting disease surveillance and RCCE activities in Afghanistan. RCCE activities include establishing a telephone health hotline, hosting health education sessions, and carrying out hygiene promotion efforts at the household and community levels.

EUROPE & EURASIA

USAID has committed $50 million to support health security, civil society, and the private sector in Italy. Providing this critical assistance will not only help the people of Italy, one of our closest and oldest allies, it will lessen the risk of cross-border spread of infection and support Italian industry. USAID's programs include the provision of essential health commodities, support for civil society and NGO partners, and support to Italian businesses to engage in research, development, or manufacturing of therapeutics, vaccines, medical equipment, and supplies related to COVID-19.

With USAID support in Azerbaijan, UNICEF produced and posted nine videos to correct misinformation—liked by more than 16,800 viewers. In addition, the UN agency produced two videos to disseminate accurate information on the virus and on how to protect against COVID-19, reaching nearly 177,400 and 206,200 viewers, respectively. The partner also created science videos to increase children's curiosity and interest in what COVID-19 looks like and on physical distancing, reaching more than 4,300 viewers.

On 9 June, USAID's partner UNICEF delivered 12,270 liters of antiseptic solution to health facilities in all regions of Belarus based on community requests, reaching up to 10,000 medical professionals across the country.

With USAID support, the German Marshall Fund (GMF) is providing small grant support through its affiliated trusts—the Black Sea Trust, the Balkan Trust for Democracy, and the Fund for Belarus—to civil society and media groups in USAID mission presence and non-presence countries in the Balkans to prepare for, mitigate, and address democratic backsliding that may occur as a result of the COVID-19 pandemic. Specifically, GMF is providing direct support to CSOs to address issues related to citizen engagement and connectivity, independent media and investigative journalism, and citizen participation in and oversight of the governance process. GMF is enhancing regional cooperation by documenting and sharing best practices in civic engagement, independent media support, and citizen-led governance responses related to COVID-19. Since May, the affiliated trusts have re-granted nearly $1 million to local organizations in line with the described activities.

LATIN AMERICA & THE CARIBBEAN

In Guatemala, JHU trained the members of 10 clean clinic commissions—groups tasked with upholding infection prevention and control best practices—as part of the national Clean Clinic Approach to improve infection prevention and control practices in health facilities such as referral hospitals and specialized centers for maternity and emergency care. This effort will help ensure many of Guatemala's frontline health professionals are better equipped to respond to the COVID-19 outbreak.

With USAID funding in Haiti, UNICEF installed more than 3,570 handwashing stations in markets, bus stations, religious centers, water points, and other critical locations in 10 target departments. These stations allow more than 1 million people to wash their hands as a key measure in preventing the spread of COVID-19.

In response to the ongoing COVID-19 outbreak in El Salvador, Save the Children is conducting RCCE activities and distributing WASH supplies with $600,000 in USAID support. The NGO is engaging national and local health authorities in six municipalities to support health promoters and raise community awareness of COVID-19 prevention measures through radio and social media campaigns. Save the Children is also distributing handwashing kits and other hygiene supplies to vulnerable households, as well as providing remote psychosocial support services to individuals affected by COVID-19.

In Jamaica, USAID is partnering with communities, civil society organizations, government agencies, and private sector entities to increase access to financing for micro-startups and entrepreneurs as well as provide vulnerable youth, families, and communities with social welfare support for lost livelihoods. These programs are augmenting the Government of Jamaica's COVID-19 social welfare programs and further building resilience throughout the country.

MIDDLE EAST & NORTH AFRICA

In Morocco, with USAID funding, UNICEF has reached more than 14 million Moroccans through risk communication activities by a variety of communication channels. For example, UNICEF's online initiative "Rendez-vous de l'UNICEF" supported by USAID funding covered various topics related to school orientation and youth engagement in the context of COVID-19, reaching more than 6 million people. Furthermore, to reinforce risk communication efforts in Morocco, UNICEF is poised to launch a new social media campaign "Vivre avec la Covid-19". The campaign will build upon previous initiatives to strengthen behavior change messaging for improved compliance with prevention measures, mobilizing youth influencers and organizations to co-create and co-implement awareness raising activities.

COVID-19 Global Response Strategy

In responding to the COVID-19 pandemic, USAID, together with DoS, launched the Strategy for Supplemental Funding to Prevent, Prepare for, and Respond to Coronavirus Abroad. Through four interrelated pillars, DoS and USAID are working to:

1. Protect American citizens and the U.S. Government (USG) community overseas, facilitate the continuation of USG work overseas, and communicate effectively;
2. Prevent, prepare for, respond to, and bolster health institutions to address the COVID-19 pandemic and the possible re-emergence of the disease;
3. Prevent, prepare for, and respond to COVID-19 in existing complex emergency settings and address the potential humanitarian consequences of the pandemic; and
4. Prepare for, mitigate, and address second-order economic, security, stabilization, and governance impacts of COVID-19.

To achieve these interrelated objectives, USAID is tailoring assistance based on country capacity and reported needs through implementation of the USG Action Plan to Support the International Response to COVID-19 (SAFER Action Plan). The SAFER Action Plan is focused on scaling up community approaches to slow the spread of COVID-19; addressing critical needs of health care facilities, health care workers, and patients; identifying, investigating, and responding to COVID-19 cases through expanded disease detection and surveillance mechanisms; employing strategies to address second-order impacts of COVID-19; and developing plans for the utilization of therapeutics, vaccines, and other life-saving supplies.

USAID coordinates with DoS, the U.S. Centers for Disease Control and Prevention, and other interagency partners to prioritize countries to receive funding for the COVID-19 response and works closely with various stakeholders, including DoS and USAID country staff, to select the most appropriate mechanisms to fill identified response gaps. USAID is also collaborating with governments, multilateral organizations, NGOs, the private sector, and other actors working on the ground to support the COVID-19 response.

Additional Information

The most effective way people can assist relief efforts is by making cash contributions to organizations that are conducting relief operations. USAID encourages cash donations because they allow aid professionals to procure the exact items needed; can be transferred quickly and without transportation costs; support the economy of the disaster-stricken region; and ensure culturally, dietarily, and environmentally appropriate assistance.

- More information can be found at USAID Center for International Disaster Information: www.cidi.org (link is external).

USAID has established an inbox (COVID19TF_PSE@usaid.gov) to coordinate private sector engagement around the COVID-19 response. In addition, the UN supports an initiative for businesses seeking to donate money, goods, or services. Please visit connectingbusiness.org for more information.

Finally, USAID reminds the public that it may accept unsolicited applications and proposals. The Agency has set up a COVID-19 Concepts portal at: https://www.usaid.gov/coronavirus/funding-requests-unsolicited-proposals.

Appendix- 6

How does COVID-19 spread between people?

20 October 2020

COVID-19 is caused by the SARS-CoV-2 virus, which spreads between people, mainly when an infected person is in close contact with another person.

The virus can spread from an infected person's mouth or nose in small liquid particles when they cough, sneeze, speak, sing or breathe heavily. These liquid particles are different sizes, ranging from larger 'respiratory droplets' to smaller 'aerosols'.

Other people can catch COVID-19 when the virus gets into their mouth, nose or eyes, which is more likely to happen when people are in direct or close contact (less than 1 metre apart) with an infected person.

Current evidence suggests that the main way the virus spreads is by respiratory droplets among people who are in close contact with each other.

Aerosol transmission can occur in specific settings, particularly in indoor, crowded and inadequately ventilated spaces, where infected person(s) spend long periods of time with others, such as restaurants, choir practices, fitness classes, nightclubs, offices and/or places of worship. More studies are underway to better understand the conditions in which aerosol transmission is occurring outside of medical facilities where specific medical procedures, called aerosol generating procedures, are conducted.

The virus can also spread after infected people sneeze, cough on, or touch surfaces, or objects, such as tables, doorknobs and handrails. Other people may become infected by touching these contaminated surfaces, then touching their eyes, noses or mouths without having cleaned their hands first.

Source: https://www.who.int/emergencies/diseases/novel-coronavirus-2019/ques-tion-and-answers-hub/q-a-detail/coronavirus-disease-covid-19-how-is-it-trans-mitted

Index

U

V

W

Printed in the USA
CPSIA information can be obtained
at www.ICGtesting.com
LVHW051056220224
772553LV00022B/164